Transplants

An Immigration Encounter of East and West

Dutch Tulips and Oriental Poppies

by

Amy J. Van Ooyen

Transplants
An Immigration Encounter of East and West
Dutch Tulips and Oriental Poppies
by
Amy J. Van Ooyen

Woodpecker Books Press

1st Printing 1998

Library of Congress Copyright Pending
ISBN # 1-889363-03-0

Printed by
BookCrafters
P.O Box 370
Chelsea, MI 48118

For our children and their children who by God's plan were transplanted from the East and West to the United States of America.

Jeremiah 29:11

In Appreciation

The age of high tech science bypassed our secluded home in the forest. I confess to writing longhand and with an erasable pen. I thank my friend Myrt Anderson who has accomplished the nearly impossible task of unscrambling my scribbled words and sentences. She and her husband Ed receive my heartfelt appreciation for their encouraging advice and concern in compiling the manuscript. Ed, your effort of inserting the photos at the proper pages is a work of art.

I thank our daughters, Judy Van der Woude for editing each chapter and Amy Greving for doing the art work on the cover.

The cover picture is the artistic talent of Gerald Kinnunen, Modern Portrait, Ironwood.

Others I must thank are Mr. Patrick O'Neil, professor of creative writing at Gogebic Community College and Georgiana Ives for doing the proofreading.

Also Susan Gustafson, Chief Director of editing for Pheifer and Hamilton Publishing in Duluth for her advice.

It is with your assistance that I present my book to our children and you the readers.

Sincerely, a transplant.
Amy J. Van Ooyen

Foreword

This is the story of how one woman came to this country from Holland with her husband and four children at the age of twenty-nine. They had three more children by birth and adopted four from Korea. Incredibly this book was written by Amy Van Ooyen who had not spoken a word of English before she immigrated to the United States.

The book tells how she coped with her motley crew, yet managed to wade a jungle stream in the Philippines, have tea with the Queen in Thailand, learn bee-keeping, and drive a school bus for fifteen years to help put her children through college.

Like so many others, they fell in love with the U.P. of Michigan and found a new life in the forest near Lake Superior, a life of joy and blessedness.

Cully Gage
Charles Gage Van Riper PhD
Western Michigan University
Kalamazoo, Michigan

Translation of Frisian Words

Pake: Grandfather
Beppe: Grandmother
Heit: Father
Mem: Mother
Tante: Aunt
Klomp: Wooden shoe
Schouw: Flat bottom boat with two swords
             replacing a keel
Welterusten: Rest well

Table of Contents

The Heart of Six Generations

Transplants

*T*he old hemlock, enjoying her trick, shook with silent laughter. A glob of snow landed on my head and the wind whispering in her branches said, "Got you again!" The cold trickle running down my back made me shiver.

"You're naughty!" I scolded. She should have more respect for me, for I am her only friend.

The old hemlock tree stands close to our home in the woods near Lake Superior in the Upper Peninsula of Michigan. Sensible men who consider her to be in the way threaten her, an impractical woman protects her. I've loved her since we came to live here. She's crooked and has lost her crown a long time ago, after which she sprouted some new branches. It makes her look stubby and fat.

When temperatures drop to twenty-five or thirty degrees below zero, my hemlock groans and pops. Her skin splits from top to bottom, but she has guts. In the spring she heals herself and her greening branches wave gently in the golden sunlight. My hemlock has a love for life.

The heavy equipment that cleared our home site laid bare some of her roots and she heard men curse her presence. Yet she shelters all who come to her; birds, chipmunks, noisy red squirrels, deer mice, tiny creeping creatures and our family and friends who come to visit us.

Since 1978, Claude and I have enjoyed living in our home in the woods. Now we decided to visit the Netherlands, our homeland. We planned to make one last trip to say farewell to the family and friends we left behind in 1951 when we moved to the United States with four young children under the age of five. Before we left, I wanted to walk on the beach at Lake Superior which dominates our environment up here. Every time I look out over her vast expanse, I feel humble and inspired. It may be a calm or a stormy day. The sky is sometimes blue or heavy with clouds, but the lake is "superior."

On one particular winter's day, I observed a colorful rainbow arching over the lake and reaching high over the trees on shore when I was in need of as-surance. It gave me great courage knowing that God is always in con-trol of our lives and our children's lives. Last night's wet snow decorat-ed the forest and a black raven cir-  cled above the lake when I left the lake's shore. Refreshed and grateful to belong to this beautiful world. I promised that we would be back.

Claude was waiting for me after he made his own pilgri-mage on the sixty acres of woodland we own. He loves the smell of the trees and is constantly planning which ones should be har-vested for firewood to heat our home in the winter. We said good-bye to our hemlock and were ready for the eight hour flight across the Atlantic. Compared to eight stormy days in 1951, the trip was exceptionally smooth. When we listened to the Dutch the flight at-tendants spoke, we discovered that we were torn between two lan-guages. I tried to say short formal sentences in Dutch when the at-tendants demonstrated the safety precautions.

"Stoelriemen wat zyn dat?" I said.

Claude just shook his head and then said nonchalantly, "Seat belts!"

"Ja," I managed to say and we laughed excitedly in anticipation of speaking Dutch conversationally again.

When we arrived at the Amsterdam airport, we had to file through customs. For a minute, I was tempted to the lane for Dutch citizens, but decided to impress the customs agent who checks foreign passports. Speaking my best Dutch, I was pleased when he said he could not detect an American accent.

"You may proceed," he said in Dutch.

It was fun to discover the expressions that bubble spontaneously from the past. Encouraged, words came easier and faster when I greeted my brother, his wife, and their children. The graying man resembled my father, short and quick with a ready, open smile; but his brown eyes are like those of my mother, thoughtful and inquiring. We hugged and kissed and then there was nothing more to say. We were back.

We drove along the busy road built high between the canals which have carried the excess water to the North Sea for centuries. A parade of boats and ships use these waterways carrying a variety of freight. Pleasure crafts give the country a more frivolous look than it appeared when we left years ago. Houseboats line the shores. This is the Netherlands which means lowlands, a country of green farm lands and prosperous cities. The land is divided by small ditches and larger canals neatly cutting the meadows into even rectangles. Small four-blade windmills snatch the angry northwest wind, and push the harnessed water to various locks. A larger windmill with sturdy sails pumps the canals full. I was reminded of the days during World War II. In 1940, the dikes were destroyed by the Germans and two-thirds of the country was flooded. Could it happen again? The water is instantly my familiar enemy.

But sheep grazed peacefully today near the red brick homes neatly built in a row. Lace curtains and bright flowers displayed behind shining windows brought cheer to a cloudy day. I saw my country with the eyes of a tourist, my heart desperately wanting to belong, but I knew I was not part of it anymore. Tears began to flow. My heart pumped like a little windmill as I tried to be brave. I remembered that Dutch people don't show their emotions and don't cry easily.

The Church: Center of a Town

We finally arrived in the town where my brother lives. The church steeple rises high above the houses clustered around it. The ambitious Dutch have utilized every opportunity. Made rich by the oil and gas industries, all of Holland is a showplace.

At my brother's home, the coffee smelled delicious and we talked, but did we really communicate? Did we understand each other? We had the same roots. Not until the midday meal was served and my brother gave thanks for our safe arrival, did I recognize my father's devotion. The intonation in his voice was so familiar and like my father's "amen" came deep from his heart. We had come from a different world, but we had the same loving God.

Yet I am a transplant. Can one's roots be in two places? The old hemlock seems too far away with an ocean in between the quiet woods near Lake Superior. Can my roots grow deeper in the Upper Peninsula soil and endure like the hemlock?

The Wedding

May 6, 1920 should have been a happy day for my parents. Jacob Hoekstra and Tryntje van der Wal had waited five long years before they could marry. But even today, when they entered mother's plain church, both were carrying a burden. Mother's family had separated from the old Reformed denomination and were now worshiping, morning and again in the afternoon, in a converted creamery.

My father had joined her, leaving the traditional State church of the Netherlands against his mother's wish. She had indicated that by withdrawing from the faith, he would, as the older son, lose his birthright to inherit the family bakery. She told him, "The people living in our conservative town will not buy your bread, not from a man who on Sundays will pass our church and take his family to worship elsewhere."

For centuries the Hoekstra families were customarily present in the large church buildings with their steeples rising to the sky in the somber Frisian country side. The men sat separately from the women, divided by a long aisle ending in front of the pulpit. Here the poor were free to sit on a couple rows of chairs. The well-to-do folks rented their pew and the very important members were privileged to occupy a raised pew enclosed by a small door.

Two luxurious benches, covered by a carved roof and placed across the pulpit against the wall, belonged to the family Ipee, the elite landowners and beneficiaries in the community. My grandparents rented pews with doors, giving the family a special status of prosperity.

Today my grandparents, to their amazement, found themselves sitting on a plain pine bench of a "Little" church, witnessing their son's wedding.

Grandma Hoekstra was the central figure in her family, wearing her beautiful Frisian costume with her golden headpiece

The "Little" Church

and its engraved ornaments covering her ears. A sunbeam glittered the gold, tempered by a fine white crocheted cap, decorated further with piped lace. Red coral beads, contrasting with her black silk dress, our Frisian Beppe (Grandma) presented herself in full regalia. Nobody expected that she felt very uncomfortable sitting next to her husband. "An impossible improper situation," she thought.

My grandfather (Pake), a good natured man, was rather amused. He kept a good distance between himself and his wife, afraid the enormous black ostrich feather of Beppe's very small hat might tickle his large nose, a Hoekstra characteristic, and it might make him sneeze.

Watching his son proudly enter the church with Tryntje on his arm, he was pleased. It was not that they disliked her, except she did belong to a different church. He already loved her as a daughter.

My father forgot for this moment that he was to exchange the family business for the girl he loved. His mother had decided the second son, his brother Jacobus, would have to inherit the bakery. Although reluctant, she had agreed to her husband's suggestion that Jacob receive a ten thousand guilder loan and buy his own business. They had decided to settle not in Friesland, but in the Province of Groningen, a few miles across the border in Lutjegast.

It had been a painful struggle between two young people who promised to begin life together as virgins. Tryntje carried her own burden as she sat down in the front pew. She prayed, " I must forgive him--I must forgive my father, but Lord, he betrayed me."

In her dark brown eyes glowed a fire and pressing her lips tightly to conceal her anguish, she still felt the shame when a teller at the bank told her, "Your father withdrew all your savings, your account is closed."

During the five long years, she had saved the seven hundred guilders, planning to buy the furnishings for her home with the hard earned money from teaching the often unruly teenagers. Earning five guilders weekly, she gave half of that to her parents.

Had she not planned with her students at the girl's school to sew her own wedding dress, even making it a class project? They had poured over the latest fashion magazines planning. The giggling girls asked her too often why the wedding was again postponed.

She would have to explain, "Not yet, we haven't set the date for sure."

Tryntje glanced sideways at Jacob. Although she was just as tall, today, he looked much shorter in his worn confirmation suit. Cramped at his broad shoulders, the black suit had a faded green shine from being aired many times at spring cleaning.

His mother Janke Hoekstra had told him, "If you are not going to marry in our church, this suit is good enough."

Tryntje was angry! Today she was wearing her Sunday dress, altered with new lace. Telling her students there was not money for a wedding dress was another disgrace, besides taking charity from her mother-in -law. She gave her a large old-fashioned commode and an old round kitchen table with caned chairs. This she had considered sufficient. Jacob decided they should buy a set of cheap dining room furniture to use on Sundays and for visiting relatives.

She will forget, she will. Someday I will try to pay her back, Roel van der Wal thought.

My mother's father fumbled with the silver knob of his shiny black cane. A flamboyant man, he loved to be noticed. Wearing the latest style clothes of his day, his white straw hat balancing on his knee and whisking a lock of dark curly hair from his forehead, he looked pleased. His feisty red-haired daughter today married a young business man. She had a streak of the artist like him, with the stubborn nature of his wife, and she was very religious. Roel, a house painter by trade, loved colors and would rather capture the bizarre patterns of marble or copy fine exotic wood. The painting of homes was boring for him and for his specialty, decorating the houses of the rich, there was hardly ever a request. The family was poor, but rich in talent.

His wife was sickly, disappointed in her life.   She mostly retreated to her own room, reading the Bible or softly singing her favorite hymns.

Roel filled his spare time directing the town's choir and small choral groups where all his children took parts. Harmony in colors and music were the love of his life.

Roel van der Wal looked at the serious couple sitting in front of him and the Hoekstra family in the next pew, a song dancing in his heart.

Oh yes, Tryntje will understand, he thought. She'll keep it quiet for her mother too. Remembering his wife, Ymkje did not concern him much. He was resigned to her situation.

Almost impatient, Roel's beautiful voice harmonized with the congregation singing one of the one hundred and fifty old Genevan Psalms, the only hymns his church allowed. The old organ could hardly cough up a tune, but Roel's rich tenor gave a sparkle to the singing, his daughter Tryntje, choking in her tears, was voiceless. "Lord, I must forgive my Father," she said again.

She stood erect and angry in front of the pulpit when the kind old pastor had asked the couple to rise. My father Jacob, in a trance rose. He thought, I will bake myself rich, for Tryntje, my wife, and give her what she deserves. My brother Jacobus may inherit the bakery but mother will probably still make all his financial decisions.

His love for Tryntje made him turn to her, and when the pastor asked him the age old questions of love and obedience, caring in sickness and health, for richer and poorer, my father proudly answered, "Yeah, ik will (I will.)" Taking my mother Tryntje, he gave her all what he had, himself.

And Tryntje, trusting in his promise, with the help of God, committed her burden to the Lord.

My parents, kneeling in front of the altar on the red velvet cushion listened reverently when the family, friends, and relatives prayerfully sang,

Because the Lord our God is good,
His mercy is forever sure.
His truth at all times firmly stood,
And shall from end to end endure.

During the singing, the gray-haired pastor descended from the pulpit reminding them of the text my mother had chosen for her wedding. "I and my house, we will serve the Lord." Joshua 24:15. He then gave, as a trusted friend of the family, God's blessing.

Tears, a stream of tears, relieved all my mother's anxiety; and smiling through her misty eyes, she watched my father's younger brother, Onne, dash past his parents, kiss her and say, "Tryntje, I always wished for a sister and today I received you!" Until the end of her life, fifty five years after she was married, he had a special place in her heart.

The wedding text my mother chose, painted on black velvet in silver letters with a small bouquet of blue violets on one corner, for years hung on the wall of our kitchen. The silver letters faded, but they kept the promise. "As for me and my house, we will serve the Lord."

It is very difficult for a stubborn Frisian girl to pretend. My mother did not wear a beautiful gown on her wedding day. Maybe that is the reason we don't have a picture of my parents taken on that day. Could it be she hoped to forget?

Engagement Picture
of
Jacob Hoekstra and Tryntje Vander Wall

Born in a Bedcloset

T he hardy Dutch do not heat their bedrooms. When I was visiting my brother, the dampness of a moderate sea climate invading his home kept me shivering between the cold clammy sheets. I longed for the cozy warm bedclosets of the home where I was born.

The old house with the bakery annex dated back to the early sixteenth century, approximately ANNO 1638. It had no bedrooms, the beds were built into the walls of our house. During the daytime, double closet doors hid the neatly made beds.

When Mother tucked us under a bright flowered quilt, she left one door partly open and the light above the living room table left a soft reflection on the whitewashed walls of the bedcloset on which my sister and I created a shadow play, a horror show with bucking goats, witches and long tailed cats using hands and fingers. It lasted until we dozed off or the awful sound effects had Mother warning us, "I'll close the doors if you don't go to sleep immediately."

"Yes, Mem," we giggled and then were quiet because we were sure she would isolate us from the family. Our feather beds were warm like a bird's nest, but with the doors closed we could not listen to the quiet conversation of our parents. We lost the privilege of belonging, not only to the family but also the community.

Hearing the adults talk, we learned the Vrouw Hamstra again expected a visit from the stork and right now she could hardly pay the bills. "Her children sleep three to a bed," my father told my mother. She had asked him to have patience. "She will pay. It's been a long winter for them. But don't give her credit for cookies and honey cake." Mother warned, knowing my father had a soft spot for children.

They said more in a whisper. To be sure we were not listening she'd ask, "Are you sleeping, girls?"

I strained my ears, not wanting to miss a word they said.

"This will now be number fourteen," Mother said. "That man should work harder. He'd be too tired for such." She made my father laugh. He loved my mother's temper. With her dark brown eyes flashing, "Mem" was a crusader for the underdog. Not understanding their argument, I dozed off, glad that there were not three in our bed. We had enough trouble pulling on blankets and fighting for space.

We spoke the Frisian language. Frisians are a proud and independent race. My parents, having been exiled for their faith into the province of Groningen, instilled in us the love for their homeland. It has had a longer literary tradition than German or English although it still shares characteristics with both. St. Boniface, murdered by the Frisians, was not a martyr for his faith, but he offended them by saying Frisians had a speech impediment.

We loved to hear our Mem sing the old melancholy melodies of their "Heitelan," accompanied by Heit on our reed organ. And it was my Heit who would take me for a walk in the evening, telling me of my birth. "You were the first girl born to a Hoekstra in four generations, Imerke," he said. "It was not easy for Mem. The doctor was glad our bedclosets are large because he had to use his instruments. When I heard your first cry, I shed tears of happiness. It was on a Friday morning at eight o'clock. It is the busiest day of the week for me, but I rushed from home and entered your name in our wedding record at the county seat. Then I rode my bike to Friesland telling our parents the news. When I came home late in the evening, I quickly went to your little basket, parted the pink curtains, and yes, you were there."

It was my Heit who told me on those evening walks where to find the north star and the constellations. "Remember, wherever you go in the northern hemisphere, you will see the same north star to guide you," he'd say. I've found a comfort in that. When in strange places and lonely, I looked for that star.

In our little village, the low German dialect was the common language. We children quickly learned to switch from our Frisian mother tongue for fear our friends would make fun of us. My mother decided she could not learn the dialect, so compromising, she spoke the high Dutch. It left her somewhat lonely and isolated since only our dominee (pastor) and the principal of the school conversed in perfect Netherlands.

Although I spoke the dialect without an accent, some of my playmates would tease me because I called my parents "Heit and Mem", and the confrontation sometimes became nasty. Many times a fight was settled with my "klomp!" Coming home in one stocking foot, carrying the cracked wooden shoe was always a humiliating experience. How was I going to explain to my angry Mem that "klomp" was broken in defense of my "Heit and Mem?" Didn't she herself refuse to speak the town's dialect? We were proud Frisians, had many friends and yet we were different and maybe a little too proud.

We were sure our father was the best baker in town. Not only did he use the best ingredients and add a little extra sugar, he also baked with real butter and honey. The best proof of it was the gold medal presented to him by Queen Wilhelmina, a great honor which he received at a baker's convention in Utrecht. The medal was displayed prominently in a showcase against a background of royal blue velvet, along with other trophies. It was also on the bread wrapping and I was taught to tear the paper so that the complete medal showed. I made sure I did, because it was my honor too. Our pillowcases made of flour sacks faintly showed the letters "Gold Medal" in a bright red circle. We didn't read English and never associated that brand name with my father's distinction.

The honor did restore my father's reputation with his parents, Pake and Beppe Hoekstra in Friesland. On one of our evening walks, he confided to me. "I lost the right to the family bakery but our queen gave me a gold medal. He then told me, "And I gave you, my four children, the most beautiful Mem in the world."

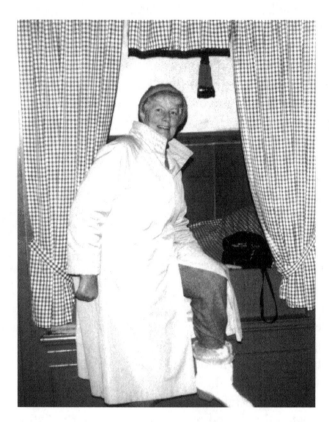

After Fifty Years
A Return to the Bedcloset

Tante Aaltje

A beam of sunlight set on fire the orange blossoms of an amaryllis on the windowsill. On the far end of the kitchen table a little kerosene tea warmer, the wick needing trimming, sputtered for attention.

Tante (Aunt) Aaltje, pouring hot tea on a lump of crystal candy sugar for my father, sighed. The crackling of the hard crystal candy was a Sunday afternoon treat and so was my safe place of sitting on my Father's knee.

"Yes Jacob," Tante sighed again. She looked at me and did not finish her sentence.

The day my father brought me to Tante Aaltje, who took care of Beppe (Grandma), was when my memory begins.

Heit (Father) puffed on a fresh cigar he had selected carefully from Tante's special cannister. "Thanks Aal," he had said. He smelled it before he lit up, again like a Sunday afternoon at home.

In the warm environment of Tante's quiet kitchen, I heard the worried adults talking. I peeked through a slit of my eyelids and made the sunbeam dance against the pretty porcelain flower pot, that held the amaryllis, its dark green glaze contrasting with the huge pink decorative embossed roses.

"Well, I have to go home, Aal, my Vrouw (Woman) is waiting," Heit said, lifting me from his knee to a chair.

Surprised, I looked at Tante who said, "Now, say good-bye to Heit, Ymkje."

He bent over me and gave me a wet kiss, the grip of his hand was too tight and heavy on my tiny shoulder. I wiggled free and wiped my face, "Yech"!

For almost four years I was Tante Aaltje's girl, the child she did not conceive because she was an Old Maid. Mem's (Mother) older sister cared for her mother Beppe Ymkje Van der Wal, who was separated from her family, bedridden in a small room. Tante Aaltje had taken her place. At age fourteen, she raised the five younger children until they were married. Like my father today, they all depended on her for help and advice.

I was too young to understand his decision to take his active inquisitive two-and-a-half year old daughter to his sister-in-law. I happily waved good-bye as he swung his leg over the seat of his bike and rode the 13 km home. He must have sadly missed me sitting in front of him on the cushioned bar. And he would miss me even more when he formed the loaves of dough with me chattering and asking questions. He often gave me a small piece of spungy dough and a few raisins to make eyes and a belly button for my personal dough boy.

Tante Aaltje's kitchen was light and cheery, the red maple chairs with rush reed seats lining up against the doors of a bedcloset. When it was bed time she helped me undress, pulling a new flannel nightshirt over my head. "Now say good night to Beppe," she said.

"Beppe?" I forgot. A very old woman lay in a huge bed supported by a stack of feather pillows. It was very quiet in that cold room. A Frisian clock on the wall with brass weights ticked loudly, "Tick, tock, tick, tock!" I shivered and quickly said, "Welterusten Beppe," and slipped out to the friendly kitchen.

The bedcloset doors were open and Tante tucked me securely under a bright red quilt. She did not kiss me good night, but left both bedcloset doors open. In the morning I awoke and found myself warmly nestled behind Tante's broad back. Sometimes she was up and I listened to the kettle with tea water singing on the four wick kerosene heater.

After breakfast of a slice of dark rye bread with brown sugar and a rusk with cheese, she dressed me. She washed my face with warm water and a soft red striped towel, so different from the stiff rough terry cloth I was used to. She brushed my long hair patiently, unlike the maid at home, who used a big black comb and pulled on the snarls until I screamed. Tante tightly braided the strands so it would not come loose on the end, tying a piece of stretched elastic. On Sundays, I would wear my pretty pink silk ribbons. "You have beautiful hair," she told me. "I wished to have only one of your thick braids."

One morning when she had taken a long time, I became impatient and told her, "You may have a braid Tante, and then you must always wear a pink ribbon. When I am grown up and you are a Beppe, I will take care of you. I will make you a pink dress too." She looked so drab in her somber clothes and I pictured a young and happy Beppe.

"No!" she said. "I will never be a Beppe."

"Yes! You will, I'll make you a Beppe," I argued, stamping my foot because I didn't want to let go of my dream. She held tightly onto my braid.

"Be quiet!" she scolded. "You are a fool child."

I pouted, feeling humiliated and forlorn. Tante behaved as if I were a stranger.

To support herself, she had a small store with anything a housewife needed in her daily life, from polish to brooms and brushes, thick cotton towels to mop the floor and linen ones for drying dishes, or lamb leather chamois for polishing windows. There were also daily earthenware dishes and washbasins besides some very expensive porcelain and crystal.

The plain dishes, pots and pans came in sturdy wicker baskets with the delivery man in a truck, the fine china and crystal by canal boat at the harbor. Those cone shaped baskets were tall, with their treasures wrapped in tissue papers hidden between strands of wood shavings.

Helping Tante was like a giant grab bag, one never knew the next precious find. It took days to reach the bottom, and she did not have to warn me to be careful. I was. The reward came when she told me to choose one little teacup for my own. I thought only one was special, a deep purple tiny cup and saucer with a black and white rim. There would not be another so beautiful in all the world. I still have it, it is broken from the transfer to America, but it does not matter. When I see it, I touch Tante Aaltje.

Tante made me feel needed. I was to shake the tightly woven black and red wool rugs and beat the heavy coco door mats. She let me go to Hinke in her little store behind a small canal for salt or vinegar. Sometimes I carried the blue enamel soap holder and Hinke filled it with soft glycerin soap. She had a scale hanging from the low ceiling and balanced the pot with shiny black and white rocks, then scooped with a wooden ladle and filled the container.

It was quite a walk but shorter by going over a single plank footbridge with one railing. They warned me never to do so or Mr. Schepel, the policeman, would take me. Schepel had our respect. Riding his bike, surveilling the town, he grew fat. We never passed his home but walked on the opposite side of the street.

"Hinke does not go to church," Tante said. She did not socialize at all. She had a huge humpback, but in her own domain she was a queen. Her white and black rocks on the counter, jewels and the fragrance of soap, vinegar and cinnamon were richer than that of the most expensive perfume.

The 31st of August, "Orange Day" and the Queen Wilhelmina's birthday, is a more important feast than Christmas or St. Nicolas Day in the Netherlands. Dressed in their very best clothes, everyone wears an orange button or ribbon. Flags wave with an orange banner from churches, buildings, farms and homes. In the morning the town's band riding on a decorated hay wagon, heads the parade, playing national songs and anthems and is followed by the children on decorated bikes and anything that can be pulled or pushed.

Farmers take their finest buggies from the barn and the horses are decked out in plumed harnesses. Next come the farm wagons pulled by work horses. For one day they are converted to covered wagons with arches of purple heather and golden yellow brembush. That day all the girls wear white dresses with a broad orange sash around the waist tied with a big bow in the back. Boys in white shirts wear an orange sash across the chest. All of Holland sings.

In Lutjegast, we had "Orange feast" too, but not like Friesland. Tante stopped one of the covered wagons. She lifted me up, and someone caught me. Waving a small flag, I rode next to the driver. It took hours before we finished the route through town and some of the countryside, but we were treated to raisin buns and hot chocolate. I loved the triumphant return, celebrating the important occasion, carrying my little flag high and shouting, "ORANJE BOVEN!"

The next day Tante said, "I need a pound of sugar from Hinke's store." I am sure now she tried to keep me busy. I thought of taking the short cut but stopped. A strange parade came down the road; two black horses covered with a black velvet tassled blanket pulled a black wagon.

On the wagon with black curtains rode a coachman also dressed in black and wearing a black top hat. Behind the wagon, two by two, men walked, dressed in black. The women came next, black veils covering their faces. They slowly came closer and the church bell started to ring, slow and loud, "Bonk..., bonk..., bonk!"-not at all like yesterday when they were clinging happily, clapping "dingely, ding, cling."

Closer they came, and I thought they had come to get me. I was to ride that awful wagon; and running in panic to Tante who peeked from behind the curtain, I screamed, "Oh Tante, here comes a horrible parade, I don't want to ride in that wagon. Please! Please?"

"It's Sietse Hiemstra. They'll hear you holler. Don't you know he died? We must be quiet and respect death." Finally the church bell, having told the years of Sietse's life, Bonk!...Bonk!, seventy-eight times was silent.

I didn't dare ask questions but woke up at night. Again, there was the black parade. Not until Tante lay in bed with me did I feel safe.

On rainy days, Tante brought big books with samples of wallpaper from which I cut roses and landscapes. Her kitchen was always warm and days were mostly sunny. Sparrows sung under the windows happily as nowhere else. And on Sunday afternoons I did not need to nap. Tante took the old green velvet photo album with decorative metal corners from a drawer. And for each picture, she had a story.

There was a photo of my great grandmother, a plain woman pictured with two Aaltjes named after her. But there was no picture of my great grandfather, Pieter Van Ooyen. He was a very devout man who believed the biblical adage you may "not take an image of anything on the earth or under the earth." We will never know what he looked like. There also was a picture of Pake, grandfather Roel Van der Wal. He dressed sharp in a dark suit, loosely wearing a white straw hat on his thick curly hair, and he nonchalantly balanced a cane with a silver knob, leaning against a fancy table.

Great Grandmother Aaltje Bouwsma Van Ooyen with grandaughters Aaltje Van der Wall and Aaltje Van Ooyen

Tante said that Grandpa was a good looking man. He liked to socialize and drank too much sometimes. One day he came home late from the tavern where someone paid him for a painting job. He stumbled and fell, missing a basin with hot boiling linseed oil he used to fabricate his own paints. When he sobered up, he knew God had protected him from burning to death. He vowed never to drink again and he didn't! "He confessed in front of the elders in church and to me," Tante said. "No one in the family knows, but he confided in me because he asked me to pray for him."

She sighed and paused awhile before showing me the picture of great grandpa Egbert Van der Wal. His wife was a poet and he an artist of sorts. "You must look at the pen and ink drawing he made that hangs in Beppe's room. It reads, 'In Jesus' heart my heart finds rest.' Instead of the word heart he drew a small heart, and he framed the poem with a larger heart.

In Jesus heart my heart finds rest.
I will my heart tie to His heart, it's all I need
This heart keeps me from evil,
no worldly heart will taste the joy this heart can give.

28

It is in this heart alone my heart finds life.
Oh Jesus, may I never lose your heart,
and that my soul and heart will never lose your holy heart.
In all eternity, my heart and soul will then forever praise
you.

"And then Beppe Ymkje Van Ooyen-Van der Wal was pictured in a cotton dress and striped apron. Her hair was parted under a white crocheted cap tightly held by a ribbon at her neck, and she did not smile. The woman did not look at all like Beppe with her hair neatly braided, lying in that cold room.

"Beppe had a twin brother and a stepsister too. Her sister married a game warden. Your mother is named after her. She had no children. She did not want them, and took herbs from a quack to prevent her from getting pregnant. She didn't want to get old either and dyed her hair with black shoe polish. They lived at the Haule in the woods. Her husband was a very good man. He loved flowers, but they always died because she poured kerosene on them. She threatened her husband saying that she would kill herself when he would not do what she said. One day she tried to drown herself in the rain barrel. It wasn't deep enough and she couldn't get out so he rescued her when he came home after chasing poachers." Tante told the story of that woman without much expression.

She did not know at that time that she would be the person who the family appointed to care for that sad woman too, until she died at a very old age.

Klaas Pieter Van Ooyen, Beppe's twin brother, had his family picture in the album with six daughters and three sons. All were gathered around a table with a Smyrna rug, but none were smiling.

Tante explained that her uncle Klaas was a successful business man. He did not want to be a dirt poor laborer working for a farmer, like the first Van Ooyen who came to the Netherlands escaping from a certain death during the inquisition in France. He was a Huguenot. When Napoleon conquered the Netherlands, everyone was to receive a new surname. Previously

The Klaas Van Ooyen Family

they went by the name of their fathers, except for royalty and the land owners who carried the name of their land or castle. When the officers of Napoleon arrived at the farm where he worked, to register everyone, the poor Frenchman was tending to the sheep who were lambing. The officer said, "Well, we name him Van Ooyen (from Ewen)." Many of the Dutch have odd surnames presuming this a temporary situation.

Klaas Van Ooyen decided to go in business. He bought a small canal boat with a cabin, got credit for a few pots and pans, every day dishes and household goods. Sometimes sailing, other times with the wind against him, he punted his ship through the canals, selling his merchandise to isolated farm wives. Coming to a town he waited until school was out and then threw handfuls of cheap clay marbles to the kids on the canal dike saying, "Tell your mothers Klaas Van Ooyen is waiting at the canal locks."

It was excitement of the children that brought the women out. After a few successful years he settled in a small store in Gorredyk. He supplied Tante and also others with the plain everyday pottery and dishes. Although being a well-to-do man and very shrewd, he died of heartache.

Tante, excusing herself said, "I have to see how Beppe is, didn't she bang her hammer?" That hammer's three loud knocks often called Tante Aaltje to come running.

I had not heard it, but when she returned she sniffed and wiped her eyes as she showed the pictures inserted in the next page. "These pictures are of Pieter Klaas Van Ooyen and his brother Wiebe, both died on the same day in a train wreck near Wezep on the way to Amsterdam. Pieter was married and his wife Anna expected their third child who was born a week after his father died on the 20 th of September.

Pieter was not like his father. He loved music and played the violin. He was not much of a business man. I liked my cousin Pieter; he was a gentleman. One day he told me, "Aaltje, I have found a wonderful and beautiful girl. Her father has a clothing store in Drachten. She always is dressed nicely and loves music. I think she likes me too, I would like to marry her." She is a widow now with two sons and a daughter, Klaas Pieter, Titia and Pieter Wiebe, named after the two men who lost their lives in that horrible train wreck.

With all the money their father accumulated, the Van Ooyen family felt they had lost everything. That day, Klaas Pieter, Beppe's twin brother wrote in his ledger, "September 13, 1918. Lord, what now? You will only know." And soon after he died.

I studied the face of a young man with dark hair and a neat black moustache. He had a kind face with large questioning eyes. His brother, the opposite of him, had blond curly hair, light colored eyes with a grin on a clean shaven face.

All Tante Aaltje's cousins, who were also Mem's cousins, were pictured in that book as there were the three brothers and three sisters Van der Wal, dressed strangely with a serious look for the moment. Even Tante Aaltje, my Mem, and Tante Anna did not ever seem to be happy.

I can't remember the day that I left Tante Aaltje, except it must have been after my sixth birthday on the 13th of May and school began on the 12th. This was not only the day the school year started but also moving day for every hired person who changed jobs. I do know that I asked Mem if she would tie a piece

Klaas Pieter Van Ooyen *Ymkje Van Ooyen*

Klaas and Elena Van Ooyen *Roel and Ymkje Van der Wal*

Tante Aaltje
(left)

My Mother
Tryntje
(right)

Pieter Van Ooyen
Anna Brandsme

33

of honeycakewith a red ribbon on my left wrist, like Tante Aaltje did.

Mem did not do it until she, tired of my wailing and begging, bothered to look for a string and tied the slice of honeycake to my wrist. It was no fun, nobody asked if they could have a bite. I missed the red ribbon and it did not taste like Tante's cake. Alone under the old chestnut tree, sitting in the grass beside a ditch, I picked at the treat, homesick and miserable, wishing for Tante.

For the rest of my school years, every vacation at Easter, Pentecost, the two long weeks in summer and at Christmas, I went to Tante Aaltje and Beppe. I took a rattan suitcase with my clothes, then filled to the brim with groceries and tied with a leather strap, Mem put me on the bus that passed our home and gave the driver instructions to stop in front of the house of the widow Van der Wal where Tante was waiting for me. Cousins came to welcome me; I was "little Ymkje." Another cousin two years older was "Ymkje the greatest," and there was "Ymkje of Uncle Peter." The other two were jealous of me because Tante gave me extra attention during my stay.

Returning home, I was the first child, the older sister, and often told I must be wiser and not squabble and fight with my little sister. It was difficult to find my place in the family again. I was my father's buddy. He took me fishing more often than my brother and sister, and we took long walks, just the two of us.

Beppe died when I was fifteen and Tante Aaltje chose some of her most treasured things, the old clock that tick-tocked in Beppe's room, a nice chest, a few chairs and a table, the porcelain tea service which her uncle Klaas gave Beppe when she married Roel Van der Wal, and also the heirloom jewelry.

For a few months she was a housekeeper for a man until she became deathly ill. For months she was lying sick at our home in the large bedcloset of the cold North-West room with the little angel above the arched mantel keeping watch. Beppe's Frisian clock ticked loudly on the wall: "tick, tock, tick, tock".

During World War II, clothes were wearing out and Tante, lying propped up in a day bed, kept knitting socks of recycled wool. Confined most of the time to her room, she had time to listen when I brought her most of my problems when I was in nurses training. She was the first to know that I met a special friend and said, "His name is Klaas Van Ooyen."

After many years, she opened the old green album and asked, "Does he look like his father? He must be very nice."

"He's much older than I am," I said abruptly. She did not answer, but I know when four years later I told her we planned to be married, she was very pleased. Following tradition, we named our first child Catherine-Alida, after my mother, but Tante Aaltje for love.

Tante Aaltje died after an operation that should have made her feel much better. I had an awful foreboding, and calling the hospital, I realized my Tante was to leave us. She spoke to all her brothers and sisters saying good bye, asking my husband, "Klaas, may Ymkje stay with me?" Mother and I waited and I could not believe she was dying. She asked me to make her more comfortable by changing her pillow, but she died in my arms.

A nurse brought me her purse when we left the room. "Don't cry," she said. "Read this." On a scrap of paper she had written, "Even though I walk through the valley of the shadow of death, I will fear no evil. Psalm 23:4."

It was months later that Mem told me, "I found an old love letter of a young man pleading for Tante Aaltje to marry him. It was with some letters she saved that you wrote her when a child. I burned that letter, nobody is to read it. She could have married him, the family would have managed. But you know Tante Aaltje..." was her final remark.

Yes, I did! I loved her very much and I almost made her a Beppe (Grandma). I had placed two beautiful girls in her arms and was expecting another little Van Ooyen daughter.

Almost a "Beppe"
with Kathy and Anne

The Old House

O ur big old home was built on the bend of the road, in the late
sixteenth century by the Lords of Rikkerda, who occupied a
mansion on the East side of our village in the town Lutjegast.

It was not the home a Dutch woman hoped for, still bearing
the legacy of the former owners who used it as a guest house and
tavern. Because of its location it also became a toll station, the
lords collecting road taxes when travelers came to town from the
land behind the North sea dikes.

Father liked our stately house with large rooms and high
beamed ceilings. When the northwest wind whistled and moaned
tugging at its corners, he would say, "Don't worry Mem, this house
stood here for centuries But she cringed at the eerie sounds when
the blue glazed tiles were rattling on the roof. Lying awake in the
bedcloset, I heard her sigh, sometimes mumbling a prayer, imagining she heard the ghost of Vrouwe Snackenburg.

Mother loved flowers and the cheery tap room with large windows became her sanctuary. The windowsills were loaded with plants. Her two sisters in Friesland shared that hobby and they all grew a clivia plant, having a contest annually. Counting the buds in its crown, the expectations and competition was serious. Sometimes fierce correspondence flew across the border because all three sisters were blessed with a sharp tongue and a temperamental nature. There in her sunny room, Vrouwe Snackenburg was no threat.

But one year, while rough-housing with my brother, I ruined the fun. Mother's clivia with a record of thirty six orange blossoms and buds smattered to the floor. Her face turned ashen. She did not let me clean the mess. "I do that myself!" she said. With her brown eyes flashing, the words bit like acid. She never let me forget; and I haven't as of today!

The Three Sisters Van der Wal

When our church was vacant, or we had a "pulpit exchange", the visiting minister stayed at our house. The northwest room was furnished with oak chairs and a massive square table with a red velvet throw. On the floor lay an imitation Oriental rug. A large vase on a stand, with dried cattails, and moneyplant and a few peacock feathers added to the stuffy interior. Pictures of Pake and Beppe Hoekstra, life size in an oval frame, decorated the wall. They stared stoically at a little baby angel on the top of the arched mantel. The angel's smiling face couldn't have been more comical, a contrast with the fakey, imposterous style of that room. I always wanted to ask that angel what she had heard from her high position. Had she smiled when there were important decisions made by the Lords of Rikkerda and their warring neighbors? Was she a witness when some were murdered and others escaped through the secret tunnel, the one that led from the mansion to the church and then to our house?

The "angst" my mother felt in this room and the ghost of Vrouwe Snackenburg still spooked our house. It was said she could not go further than the old church and there disappeared in the cemetery among the gravestones of the Rikkerda family. Had the tunnel caved in or was it still passable? Our little angel did not tell me; she just smiled.

Even on nights when the northwest wind did not howl over the lowlands behind the sea dikes, mother complained. "This house is never quiet." She was right, some of the mysterious noises were easily explained. They were mice scurrying behind the walls. The "tock-tockety tock" of wood worms gnawing in the old beams were the eerie forebodings of death, so the folks thought. "It is a warning that someone is going to die," Willemke, our maid said. She had many superstitions. I liked to listen to her ghost stories about Vrouwe Snackenburg.

But when the evening meal was finished and Heit asked, "Amy, will you go and get the Bible from the kitchen?", I had to be brave as the oldest child. I completed the walk back to the light warm room in a few desperate leaps. I have never asked why they kept the Bible in the kitchen when we ate in the living room, the only room that was heated later in the day.

My friends talked much about Vrouwe Snackenburg, but almost a "forboten" subject at home. Heit changed the conversation with a worried look at mother.

People thought our family was a little different. Not one of my friends had a room with a little smiling angel, or a fancy bed-closet where the visiting "dominee" slept. That cold northwest room certainly was worthy of a man of the cloth and who was not aware or disturbed by a spooky ghost.

When I was about twelve mother let me sleep there. It

was a happy and lively place. One wall separated it from the bakery where a colony of black crickets had found warm shelter. In the evening they began to fiddle a love song. The first one started with a few strokes, giving a tune, a second member followed and soon everyone joined in, playing the age old symphony of lust for life and the procreation of their species. The concert ended as it began, only one or two screeching a last note.

My First Bike

For us as children, the house had endless opportunities for play. Hide and seek was our favorite game. We could also climb the rafters in the old barn where we had our own indoor playground since we did not have livestock other than "Pietje", my father's white pony who pulled the wagon with bakery wares. She was old and raised by traveling circus folks who taught her many tricks. Pietje said "Please" and "Thank you" by nodding her head and scraping the floor with her left and right foot. She easily untied the knots in a rope and she did a dance. Once Pietje saw her image in the large window of the one general store in town. My father said, "I hated to spoil her fun, but I couldn't afford a new window."

We did have a couple of chickens housed in a stall at the end of the cow barn. Like so many farm homes, the barn is attached to the house. The "privee" as Mother called it, or our "huske", (little house) as Dad said, was also at the very end. While waiting in turn for relief, we friends would pile in the roomy chamber to poke our finger through a knothole and tempt the chickens to come running for a fat pink morsel. Even a determined poke in our fingers by the old rooster didn't spoil the fun of fooling them. Our giggles confused the grown-ups, who would chase us away when they came to call for the one holer chamber.

We played house in the hayloft and traveled far and wide in

an authentic horse drawn buggy. The brass coach lights and bright green upholstered cushions affirmed the importance of our trip and that of the owner, a rich farmer who had stored it in the barn for years.

Each season brought with it their own excitement. It was a sure sign of spring when the peddlers came to town, knocking at our door first. Their little boxes or suitcases held small articles like shiny pearl buttons on a blue card, safety pins on a pink one, shoe laces and a few yellow pencils, along with a comb or two, just a few necessities so that they were not called beggars.

Mother never bought anything. She handled something as if she would, gave them a dime and put the item back in its place. She acted as if she were an easy target but when she smelled alcohol on their breath, they found out she was no fool. Others politely asked if they could set up shop in our barn. The man who recaned chairs came with a bundle of rush reed, carrying it on his back. Leaving it in the barn, he disappeared for a couple hours, returning with an assortment of kitchen chairs. Some required a total new seat, which he wove in long strands, the front longer than the back and sides, so that it formed comfortably to one's rump. Other chairs only needed a few new strands which were then a bright green color that slowly faded.

I liked to see that. It reminded me of a neat stable family routine. All was well when the chairs were fixed again. The man used a homemade wooden needle as a tool and he must have cut the rush during the winter months when ice had formed in the canals. He chewed a lot, concentrating on his craft, and we learned to keep our distance very well.

The scissor and knife sharpener would occupy his hand cart with whetstones in the barn too, but for only one day. Walking through the village at a quick pace, the little man returned loaded with household tools that needed sharpening. We watched him when we came from school at noon for lunch. It was fascinating to see that little man pump a huge pedal with the sparks flying and the grinding noise. He was all motion, even biting on his enormous moustache. Mother did not like the man. He was not treated to hot chocolate and a raisin bun like the "caning man." She tolerated tobacco, but a shot of brandy at the local tavern was a mortal sin.

Then when all the housewives had finished spring cleaning, the ragman arrived. We couldn't go in the barn when he sorted the rags, wool, from cotton, and in smaller bags the clothes that he thought might be of use. We watched him from the wide open barn doors. He was handed his treat through a small window built in a dark kitchen closet, the one through which the coachman of the wealthy guests to the Lord of Rikkerda were once served.

"It is enough that your Heit comes home from his bread route during winter months with fleas. We don't need the other," she'd say. To be sure I had not been near him, I had my long hair combed with a very fine "nit comb." I did not like the ragman, except if we promised to stay away from him, Mem might give us a dime for a new top. We put a shiny thumb tack on the top, colored it with crayon and made our own whip, with the goal to keep it spinning until we reached school just a few blocks past both churches, the "Old" one and the "New"!

We, of course, went to the "NEW" church and to the "School with the Bible." For eight years I passed "The Other", and there was always a shaky truce between us. Each side also bought bread from their own baker. Those who went to the old church sent their children to the old school. There were more of "us" from the "new church", then of them, the "old church", but it did not help much when we got beat up.

Our spring cleaning was not finished until the outside of the house was thoroughly brushed with lye and glycerin soap, a distinct Frisian cleanliness. Our neighbors did not see the need for it, but then, they were "grimy Groningers." Mother insisted on it and all the family, even we children, stormed at the brownstone walls. I loved to rinse the soap water down. Nobody saw the difference but we were sure proud of the accomplishment.

Finally came the cleaning of the rain cistern and that created a problem. Willemke refused to go down the narrow opening of that dank cavern where she was to scoop the debris at the bottom. Trembling with fear she threatened, "I'll quit when you make me, baker Hoekstra!" She always called my father the baker. "It's too spooky," she sobbed.

It would be a disgrace when a maid quit before the twelfth of May when all the servants were hired. It was bad for her and also our family's reputation. People would talk about us.

Most people in town had a rain barrel or a cement cistern, but ours was the end of the tunnel, the little room separated by a wall of yellow brick masonry from the rest of the secret passage to the old church.

I had been curious as a child, and at one time father permitted me to go down, but Mother wearily worried and said, "That's no place for a young girl Heit." He then shrugged and we grinned as always when my mother warned cautiously, "She's a girl." I did not want to be a girl. Boys could do everything girls weren't allowed to.

Willemke pouted for a few days. Mem was worried. The cistern cleaning could not wait. A good rain storm would fill it again. She was a heavy woman so it would be impossible for her to slide through the narrow opening. Heit would not have his assistant go down, "That is not why I hired him," he said. Although my father had cleaned that cistern, he now pretended to be too busy and besides, it was really women's work. My brother was too young to be left alone four meters underground.

Mother finally, very reluctantly, gave in to my father's suggestion that I should clean the rain cistern. So with much caution and lots of advice, they lowered me through the narrow brick opening. Wearing my father's big rubber boots, a warm hat and an extra sweater, it got too hot. The neat little room down there smelled and was dark and warm. The damp catacomb looked spooky by the light of a small kerosene lantern. The green and yellow glazed tiles on the floor were covered with a layer of gook that I was to scoop with a dustpan into a pail. Then I hollered "Up!". That done, I had to scrub and rinse the walls. And finally, when I scooped all the soap water into a pail, I mopped the floor. All the while, fat drops of evaporation soaked my heavy clothing. The adults shouted instructions, Mother asking, "Are you finished?" And Heit hollered, "Here comes the ladder, ready to come up now?" I thought, "Now? It is too bad I can't stay here awhile. This is a cozy little room once it's clean."

The walls were built from centuries old "Frisian" bricks like those of the eleventh and twelfth century churches. They were eighteen inches long, eight inches wide and the tiles were like the floor in Pake and Beppe Hoekstra's church. There was no doubt in my mind that this quiet place had some ghost stories to tell. There even may be a few skeletons behind the yellow sandstone enclosure, of those who didn't escape and were murdered in flight.

I climbed the ladder and my father hoisted me to the everyday world. It was too noisy with everyone asking questions. I shivered. "You are chilled," Mem said. I did not tell her that it was warm down there. She would never have understood that the outside world was cold and scary now.

As was the custom with spring cleaning finished, we had an afternoon celebration. Heit brought a selection of little cakes and torts. Mem took the wine glasses to the table, opening one bottle each of golden sweet Rhine wine and the dark red cherry. For the children there was canned fruit served in small crystal dishes with a purple stem. Heit gave me a wink and for the first time he poured me a half glass of Rhine wine. Everyone except Willemke laughed because I was only thirteen. Sipping her wine, she suddenly burst into tears. "I am sorry Vrouw Hoekstra," she sobbed. "You don't believe me, but I heard Vrouwe SNACKENBURG down there last year!" She was now afraid to lose her job.

"Did you hear some...some...noise?" she asked me. "Did you? It is her knocking, I know! It is Vrouwe Snackenburg spooking this house!"

I shook my head when I watched Mem leaving the room. "Only a tick-tick-tick!" I said.

"That is Vrouwe Snackenburg knocking, Baker Hoekstra." Willemke's eyes were wild.

My father, more worried about Mem, tried to calm her. "Willemke," he said. "Listen to me. Down in that cistern behind the wall is the noise of water dripping from the arched ceiling of a tunnel. Please come with me and we'll talk to my Vrouw and explain."

They left our somber kitchen, finding Mem in her cheery sunny room. I never heard Willemke ever mention Vrouwe

Snackenburg again or tell a ghost story. She stayed with our family a long time until finally she got married after the twelfth of May.

After forty years, on my last trip to the Netherlands, I returned to the old house. I wanted to speak and hear the language of Heit and Mem and went to Friesland.

I crossed the border to Lutjegast in the province of Groningen. My birth place was waiting for me in the bend of the road. The stately front part had not changed, but the barn and the stables were gone, making place for a modern house.

When I opened the door of the bakery store, the northwest wind blew it shut and the sound of the bell was like it was when I was a child.

When the wife of the baker saw me, she said, "It is a miracle the window in that door does not break."

It was what my Mother would say, but the same cut glass window of that door had not broken. It was outrageously expensive, I remembered, too extravagant for a small town bakery like that gold medal given to my Father by Queen Wilhelmina.

I told the lady, "I was born in this house, in that large room in one of the bedclosets"

"Come and see, we remodeled the house," she said.

The bedclosets were now hidden by cheap paneling. She brought me to the kitchen. "We've taken out one wall and replaced the small window, " she said. That explained the reason for it now being light and friendly. "We enlarged it too, adding much of the hall. It's now a family room," she said proudly.

"Very nice." Avoiding the presence of Vrouwe Snackenburg, I said, "We used to have a rain cistern with an unusual pump, a cabinet with three brass spouts and a black marble sink."

"Oh, that one, we sold it to an antique dealer," the woman said.

"And the smaller room on the northwest?" I asked as we walked back to the store.

"We divided that into two bedrooms," she said as she took her place behind the counter. I wanted to ask her about the little angel on top of the gothic arched mantel. Had she lost her smile? But I said, "I smell fresh coarse rye bread, the dark bread without yeast my father used to bake."

"Yes, it was just delivered, it is warm yet. We only sell bread, it is baked by a warm bakery." She then explained that they were what was called a "cold" bakery.

I bought a large four pound loaf. It was warm in my hands, but I shivered. There is not a warm place here for my crickets to hide. There is not one little cricket singing tonight. The fiddlers have left. The concert has ended.

Bliksem and Thunder

"Your grandparents have come; today we have dinner in the front room." Mother, usually well composed and calm, hurried with a large bowl from the kitchen.

Pake and Beppe Hoekstra

Oh, yakkes! was my first thought.

A tall woman draped in black sat at the head of the table, my father's place.

"Amy, give Beppe a hand," mother said.

"Hello." The touch of her cold fingers were a reflection of what I saw in the look of her face.

My grandfather broke the ice by asking, "Well, Tryntje, what do we have for dinner?"

My pake's sparkling brown eyes were hinting one of the silly expressions he used for common food when he said, "So it will be parallel with my nose, and earth apples too!"

Smiling happily, he took a seat next to my father. We all relaxed. Mother's menu of potatoes and green beans with meatballs was a good choice for the elderly people used to a plain fare.

When Willemke, our maid, brought a huge chocolate pudding for dessert topped with a mountain of whipped cream, I almost forgot the chilly formality that my grandmother took with her.

"Tryntje, what is that?" Grandfather had expected a big bowl of hot rice porridge sweetened with brown sugar and tasty cinnamon.

"A pudding, chocolate pudding, Pake," my brother Piet joined by our little sister cheered. All eyes were on mother, who, cutting a portion first for the guests, then my father and finally us too, heaped more cream on our plate.

Pake, taking a spoonful of the squigly delicacy concluded, "Tryntje, this is new to me and so cold. I wish to mix it with a hot potato."

He did so, then, complimenting my mother on her good meal, said," That is exactly what it needed. Your dessert was very good."

Beppe sat at the same place when we came home from school in the afternoon. Her gold cap glittered in a beam of sunlight, the ornate wings above her ears accented a fine Belgium lace hat that softened the glare of gold.

My Frisian grandma had come to our home in the province of Gronigen in full splendor. We were well aware of her importance. My father's business depended on her money. I tried to avoid Beppe. For some unexplained reason, Beppe and I always had an unhappy confrontation.

"One's hands must be busy or the devil will make use of them," she'd say, and true to her word, she was constantly knitting. Her knitting needles clicked in a steady rhythm, clickety, click, click. A ball of unbleached cotton yarn danced at her feet. The crazy ball, freely jumping up, rolling off and returning to Beppes feet , made me laugh. Her needles clicking, click, clickety clicked on, with a tip of her tongue slipping left, right, left right, between her her thin lips.

"Beppe!" I asked. "Why does your tongue move so fast when you knit?"

"Be quiet, child. I have a job to finish," she grumbled. She never mentioned my name but would always say, "Child." I was not named after her; my younger sister Janke was, and Piet, my brother, had Pake's name.

"Amy, staring at people is very impolite." Mother made it clear, there was nothing more to question.

I had many questions and some strong feelings too.

Grandma, who was nearly blind with cataracts, knitted with a plain straight stitch making mattress pads for her four daughters-in-law. No doubt, this one nearing completion was meant for us. The ribbed pattern was uncomfortable to lay on and gave our tender buns an itch, especially this new pad that would soften after several washings. I was not sure my mother would be as pleased as she pretended with Beppe's gift. Why was I then the first one to be tortured by the "underspread," as she called the thing.

I had not heard of any friends who slept on something like it, but then, they didn't have a Frisian grandma either who wore black two piece dresses. Hiding under many layers of skirts was a huge pocket tied around her waist. I imagined it filled with money because we all received a silver guilder which she managed to dig from between her underwear.

"I trust your last report card was good?" she inquired when she handed that big coin to us.

My brother's grades were much better and I, as the older one, kept quiet.

Piet turned his guilder over and over in his hands, examining the image of Queen Wilhelmina, and did not know what to do with it.

The shiny coin was not making me happier. I knew we were supposed to drop it through the slot in a tiny gray can with a small padlock and I would never see it again. My Dad brought our savings to the school principal who twice a year had a sitting with the bank located in another town.

Mother immediately took the saving boxes to the table for Beppe to see. We plunked the heavy coin through the slot, ka-ploonk, it was gone. Vigorously shaking the can gave me some satisfaction. "Amy, you know better, you are the older one, quit that noise," mother said.

Yes, my Beppe was rich, mysteriously rich, wearing gold on her head and a triple string of red corral beads fastened by a gold lock for a necklace. They were called "Real blood coral," but what was that? The name gave me shivers. What were they? The heavy necklace had been in the family as an heirloom for many generations and her French ancestors had probably brought it to Friesland.

Not any of my friends had a rich Frisian grandma. It set us apart. Secretly proud of our heritage, I tried to compromise. I wanted to belong and caused trouble at home by speaking in front of Beppe the low dialect of our town.

It must have been on a long Easter holiday weekend that the payment on the principal and interest of the loan was due. All our family visited Pake and Beppe at Ryperkerk. On Sunday morning, we all paraded to the old Reformed church where the men sat on one side of the aisle and the women on the other.

In the front of the pulpit were a few rows of chairs for people who were too poor to rent a pew. We sat in a pew with a canopy and door reserved for the more prominent folks in town. Beppe firmly told me, "If you don't sit still, we will move you to the chairs and you are a shame to our family."

The crowded pew didn't give me a chance to wiggle and the little door was locked. This was enough of a punishment. Mother gave me an extra peppermint, and I tried to make it last by biting off little pieces, sucking them slowly. My dangling feet desperately wanted to kick the wooden casing in front of me.

Oh, what a relief when I finally ran to my grandparent's home across the little footbridge and then somersaulted on the green grass, sensing Beppe's disapproval! My brother, walking slowly with the men, tried to copy Pake, who strolled along, his hands folded behind his back.

The air smelled of young green grass growing in the wetlands, and inside my grandparents' home, was the fragrance of cured provisions. Crocks with sauerkraut and green beans were lined up near the kitchen door. Smoked sausage and bacon dried near the chimney and onions; kidney beans still in the shell hung in bunches from the ceiling with herbs and bundles of dried sage.

"Saely Molke," hot sage milk with lots of sugar, was the cure for many ills. "Saely keeps the blood thin and warms the stomach. It fights a cold; a poultice of saely leaves relieves toothaches and it kills the worms too," Pake said.

At four o'clock, cocktail hour, Pake deftly poured the brew into small porcelain cups, inviting us for a drink. The warmth of his voice made me a believer; I slurped it slowly and it felt good in my stomach.

My grandfather's hobby, among many talents, was building boats. He had a flat bottom fishing boat, a shouw with a sword on each side for sailing. The boat didn't have a keel. One could also row it or punt the boat through the canals. He had a license for fishing with nets and a cane pole. He kept his catch fresh under the seat of the boat in a creel and saved the squirmy eels he caught for a Sunday dinner. Had the fishing been very good, he would add a layer to the pickled fish in a crock in his workshop.

Pake's Homemade Shouw

Pake did not go fishing on Sundays. Nobody would; but on Monday morning he told my father, "Well, men, I must check my nets. We'll take a can of worms and our poles. Let's see what we will catch. Piet, you are big enough to hold the rope of the small sail. You can come along."

They didn't invite me, and I immediately knew why, "I am a GIRL!" not good enough to go fishing with Pake. My brother, two years younger, would go sailing in the canal between the high rush reeds where waterfowl scurried to find shelter and white waterlilies bloomed, lining the shore. "Oh, how horrible, deserted by my father and Pake who liked Piet but did not love me. Heit, who always took me fishing now let me down!"

I begged, cried and pulled on Dad's coat. Taking my brother with him, he didn't even look back. Mother tried to console me, "Amy, you will go tomorrow. You have Easter vacation and it will be your turn."

Furious, I did the unpardonable. "No!" I screamed, stamping my feet. "Beppe, you don't like me. You like Piet, he is a boy and Janke, she is named after you! I hate you! I really hate you!"

"No, I don't like you and you are not wanted in my house!" Beppe shouted.

She yanked me out of the room, pulling my braid, and dragged me to the shed in back, slamming the door shut. I heard the padlock click.

I was jailed in a dark shack smelling of tanned fishnets and much more. In one corner was the outhouse and the very distinct odor reeked; it smelled not at all like ours at home.

It began to rain, heavy drops ticked a monotone on the asphalt roof. In the distance, the thunder rumbled, at first a friendly grumbling, a warning to find shelter. An angry boom followed, making me jump from the nail keg near Pake's work bench. Lightning flashed and a horrendous loud clap shook the little building.

I was sure God too was very angry with me; a loud hissing noise, a flash of light made me cringe. "Now God is going to strike me dead! " Maybe, very maybe, He would not kill me if I sat in that stinking outhouse. Hooking the latch on the door, I waited, sitting on the worn red painted stool. I asked God to forgive me, but all I heard was His angry voice.

Because of her own fear of thunderstorms, my mother worried about me. Finding me, she bent over my crumpled form that was twitching and in shock. Drying my tears, she said, "Hush, hush, we will pack your clothes and at four o'clock we catch the bus at the highway. You may go to Tante Aaltje."

In Beppe's dreary little kitchen, she washed my face. "Now you must go to Beppe and ask her forgiveness," she said.

My shoulders were still jerking at intervals, and trying to stifle my tears, I said, "Beppe, will you forgive me?"

She sat in her padded cane chair. Looking up from her knitting she said, "No! Never! I can't, at least not now." She may have, and then, she may have not.

Mem squeezed my hand tightly and led me across the small foot bridge to the red brick paved road, telling me of the wonderful days I would spend for the rest of the week at Tante Aaltjes'. Finally my shoulders stopped jerking and she let go of her grip, I skipped along the highway.

We made a game of counting the passing cars before the bus arrived; we counted thirty-six. She kissed me good-bye, and when the bus swallowed a little eight-year-old girl, I heard her say to the driver, "Please take her to the home of widow VanderWal. My sister does not expect her."

When it was time to again pay the interest, Heit took me with him for the day. Pake made sure I was coming along to fish for a few hours. He asked me to tightly hold the rope of the sail. We levied the boat along a canal that brought us to his favorite fishing hole, a small lake called the "Grote Wielen."

Sheltered by tall rush reeds, we snacked on honey cake and "saele molke." Every time I took a bite, the bobber showed a fish biting too.

Pake said, "I'm proud of you. I will tell Beppe you are the best fishing buddy I have ever had."

It may have been the fishing hours and the fact that God adds those to the days of your life, or the Saelie Molke, but my Pake lived to his ninety-fifth birthday. He died at the home of my parents in Lutjegast, the province Gronigen. Tryntje, my mother, who for her strong faith and conviction was to leave her beloved Friesland, lovingly cared for him.

Reading the genealogy of the Hoekstra family sent to me by my cousin, Jenny Hoekstra de Veer, I realized the many talents of Pake were inherited from his intelligent ancestors who were leaders in their community. They were county judges, magistrates and already in the early 17th century, well educated. Among them were several school principals and one was an architect.

One of Pake's grandfathers is a Frenchman who came as a missionary to Zwaagwesteinde, a very poor area in East Friesland where the sandy soil barely sustained the people. After his retirement, he wrote a book with the title, "God cares for you...Love is foremost," published by the firm Schaafsma in Dokkum. Egbert J. Conradi's life was a testimony of love for the underprivileged.

Art and music came naturally to the Hoekstra's. In those days, the organ had a prominent place in society, and some were organists in two churches.

In Napoleon's time, the family took the name Hoekstra because they lived at a good sized farm on the corner (the Hoek) at the West dike to Giekerk. There is still a sign on the house that says, "Hoekje," dated from approximately 1690.

Not all of the family were saints. One of the ancestors lost his wife, and courted the daughter of a rich farmer who became pregnant. He then fell in love with the family maid and abandoned his pregnant fiancee. This was a serious crime in those days, and he was arrested. His guard of Swiss nationality fell asleep, and he had a chance to escape, disappearing with the maid. Others did not receive an education and were farmers. One Hoekstra's drinking habits caused him to lose his land; he hung himself on an apple tree.

Pake Pieter Hoekstra was more adventurous than most of his family. Receiving his teacher's degree, he decided to apply for border patrol. Smuggling was very profitable for the Germans who, avoiding the high tariffs, under cover of darkness, crossed the border by night. Pake, boarding at the home of a baker and tiring of his dreary cold and dangerous job, learned the trade and returned to Ryperkerk where he married and bought a bakery.

Pake was better as an organist and music teacher than at baking fancy cakes and cookies. He baked breads, the regular white bread, raisin bread, and sticky gooey sugar cinnamon loaves, as well as the delicious Frisian spiced cakes, chuck full with dried fruit, raisins and small bits of hard candied sugar.

Late in his life, he composed music of which we have inherited one preserved copy. It is simply named, "A Pretty Little tune of Pake" (It Moaye Wieske fen Pake). Signed 28 Dec. 1939. Pieter Hoekstra was born Dec. 31, 1862 and died Dec. 12, 1957.

Beppe Hoekstra

Pake Hoekstra

The Four Brothers Hoekstra

*The State Church Where the
Hoekstra Family Worshipped*

Church Organ Where my Grandfather and Four Sons Were Organist

Composition by Pake Hoekstra

Prelude

Nervously waiting for the elderly man, the child rotated faster and faster on the organ stool. Spiraling up and catching himself, he pivoted down to an abrupt stop.

His music teacher had told him, "Just a minute. I must first feed my cat first. It's a bossy cat and she'll pester us."

Again going to the very top, wobbling a little, the boy reversed and went down, freely swinging his skinny legs and releasing himself of the anxiety when meeting someone unfamiliar.

Claude

Since he did not have a father and was insecure, he shyly avoided the men he did not know. Most of them were serious, soberly dressed in dark suits. They payed no attention to him except when he misbehaved.

He looked at his face in the mirror in front of the old decorated reed organ. He hated his big ears and long narrow face, his dark brown eyes and his black hair; he hated himself. Why couldn't he be like the other boys in school with blond hair, blue eyes and a ruddy, round face? Why couldn't he wear a light blue shirt without a tie like everyone else in his class?

Rotating again, faster now, he forgot to catch himself; wobbling, he rolled to the floor.

Hearing a door slam and the elderly teacher coughing, the boy waited. Too ashamed to move, he just lay on the floor.

"So, you've practiced the stool. Don't worry, we'll fix it," the man told him.

Looking up, he stared, relieved to see the friendly smiling face of his new teacher.

"What's your name, son?"

"Claude Peter," he answered.

"You may call me Uncle Lutze," the elderly man said. "How old are you, Claude?"

"Six, but I'll be seven next month." Nervously, he sat down again on the organ stool, stretching his legs to reach the pedals.

"We'll practice on the organ now, but must warm our hands first," Uncle Lutze said.

Swinging his arms, jumping up and down and beating his shoulders, Uncle Lutze was laughing aloud as they exercised, greatly enjoying the child's gymnastics.

"Now, we'll practice the pedals. Can you reach them?" he asked.

The Stern Man in Dark Clothes

The boy's toes barely touched them and his fingers desperately tried to span a full octave.

His teacher encouraged him, praising his fine long fingers. "Claude, you have good hands for playing the organ. Your hands are like your father's. I taught him to play the organ too, but he was better on the violin."

The old teacher paused. Staring at the little boy, he shook his head and recovered from his memories. Then smiling kindly at the boy, he suggested, "We'll play a game. You practice the pedals. Steady now, not too fast! I'll play the keys and together we make music."

The teacher's old arthritic hands were smooth and carefully touching the white and black keys, he played a joyful prelude.

When Claude heard the warm vibrating organ tones, he forgot to pump the air and the music faltered.

"Are you tired?" his teacher asked.

Shaking his head because he had blundered again, Claude

said, "Oh, I want to play music like you Uncle Lutze."

"You will, son; someday you will," Uncle Lutze answered, his face beaming. "Now you will play the keys and I will pump."

Fast, faltering and without expression, a childish tune danced from the keyboard.

"It's not so good," the boy said. "My mother told me about notes, but I want to make music like you, Uncle Lutze."

"Come again next week," Uncle Lutze said.

He watched his young student jump off the granite stoop, and sadly shaking his head, he felt weary and tired. Coughing again, the old man remembered the other boy, Claude's father.

Claude wasn't sad. He was feeling great and big, so big he gave Uncle Lutze' black cat a scare, pretending to kick it which made the old cat run for cover.

"How was your first lesson with Uncle Lutze today?" his mother asked when he came running home.

"Dumb!" he said. "And he has a mean black cat too. But I did all right."

Still feeling confident, he looked up at his mother and demanded, "I want a blue shirt like all the other boys wear in school!" He was almost sure she would buy him one now.

Every Wednesday afternoon Uncle Lutze eagerly waited for Claude to appear. When the boy came running in for his lessons, the black cat, hissing and spitting, ran for cover again. Claude soon learned to make music, the organ responding to his young fingers with warm deep tones.

But Uncle Lutze's coughing spells got worse. Every week his shoulders drooped a little more while he was bending over the boy's slight body on the organ stool. Claude did not notice this, because Uncle Lutze's voice was always kind and the eyes of his teacher and friend always twinkled when they warmed up, jumping and slapping their hands.

Then one day, Claude's mother told him, "You will have no lesson today. Uncle Lutze is not home. He has gone to a place called a sanitarium to rest for awhile."

The boy did not understand. "No Uncle Lutze to go to on Wednesday?"

When his mother noticed his disappointment, she said, "He gave me a message for you. You must tell Claude to practice every day and make the organ sing so he can play in church for me someday."

Claude quickly wiped away a tear with the sleeve of his new bright blue cotton shirt, one like all the tough boys wore at school and went to his mother's reed organ . Rotating on the organ stool, swinging his legs faster and faster and again forgetting to stop in time, he wobbled and fell, a piece of sheet music fluttering to the floor beside him.

Anna Van Ooyen
Widow at the Age of 28

Placing it on the organ, he read the title, "There is Pain in Saying Farewell."

His mother had sung it often, accompanying herself on the organ. Slowly and carefully looking at the notes, he played the song.

Hearing his mother weep behind him he turned and saw her crying. Embarrassed, he asked himself, "Why is she angry with me? Did I play so poorly?"

She was not angry. He could not understand why that song

made her weep. He'd been too young to remember his father who had died in a train accident when Claude was only four years old.

Claude
At the Old Church Organ in the Netherlands

Interlude

For an introduction of the Sunday afternoon organ concert in one of the Hague's oldest churches, the master organist had chosen one of J. S. Bach's Preludes.

The warm organ tones thundered in mighty variations through the darkest corners of the church and had captured the appreciative audience. After a perfect performance, there is, in the Netherlands, no greater reward than to leave in silence.

One young person hidden behind a large pillar remained in the old sanctuary as if to catch the last echo of the music lingering in the church.

For Claude the sudden change from Bach's majestic choral fantasia to Handel's frivolous composition, "The Cuckoo and the Nightingale," was so unexpected. Engrossed, he still heard the joyful song of the nightingale with the Cuckoo answering, as if begging for an encore of the happy nocturnal song. Repeating again and again, the nightly duet continued in endless praise.

"I must lock the doors of this church, son," the janitor said as he touched the young man's shoulder.

As if in a trance, Claude reluctantly left. For him the concert had no end, he always would hear the call of the organ.

You Are the Older One

The older one, the older one, the older one must be wiser... I still hear an echo from the past. At thirteen, the world was gray, my dress made from mother's old coat was gray and it even had a yoke of a darker shade of gray. To lengthen the dress, mother added a border of gray on the seam. At school all the walls were painted gray and our male teacher wore a gray suit. It was a little tight on him in the crotch, and he often rearranged his pants. We girls giggled about it behind the man's back.

We were thirteen and a little smarter and would soon start a new life after graduating from the seventh grade of the School of the Bible in Lutjegast. On the last Friday morning of that school year in the second week of May, our headmaster entered the

Janke, Ymkje, Pieter
Ralph Was Not Born

65

classroom, followed by the president of the school board. I had never liked the rich farmer with an air of all importance because I knew he did not buy my father's bread. The man's ruddy face was flushed and he seemed uncomfortable. "Mr. Van Anken has to tell you about a new law," our principal said.

Eighth Grade Friends

A dull sense of something gone wrong hushed the tense class when he left in a hurry.

"Our government has decided that for those of you who are not going to continue your education, an eighth grade will be added before you will end your formal education and receive your diplomas. You all will return to school on Monday. The problem is we do not have a new curriculum for the eighth grade so you will have to repeat seventh grade this year. You are all required by law to return to school by Monday. Today you are dismissed early. Teacher, you may now end the day with prayer."

Very few students from the School of the Bible went to the big city High School. Only the children of the dominee and our school principal were planning to do so. We were old enough to work, boys at the farms or their parent's store, and girls hired out or stayed home until they married. And they had to marry a young man

50 Year Reunion
(same order)
Pietje, Marie, Ymkje, Dieuwke

of their church who was in good standing in the community.

I had secretly hoped for a miracle, but my parents made it very clear. They could not afford transportation and not even good clothes. We were still in a depression. I hated wearing the old hand-me-down sweater with a zig-zag pattern of silk woven in it. The stretched-out thing had come with a box of clothing from my aunt living near the Hague. Mother gladly accepted castoffs. "You are the older one and must be wiser. Your brother Piet will need a higher education," Mother said.

That was fuel for greater resentment for me, as a girl and as the older one!

The eighth grade would have been a total loss for me since there was not a planned curriculum, had it not been for a very tall handsome dark-haired young man who was hurriedly hired to be our teacher. Athletic and lean, he joked with the boys and flirted with us girls. We nicknamed him Mister Long Legs and fell hopelessly in love.

We had forgotten our poetry albums from fifth and sixth grade. At one time there had been a contest to see who could collect the most entries of rhymes and poetry, but we laughed about silly rhymes like the one my Uncle John wrote who tried to fool everyone.

When you once like Grand ma ma,
Cozy sit next Grand pa pa.
Pondering about old times
I hope you keep me in mind.

And we made fun of the serious poems and verses of our parents and teachers. Some of the girls had beautiful velvet albums with pictures of angels on clouds of silk and cherubs carrying a bouquet of Forget Me Nots. I was not so lucky. My album was plain with a brown gray cover.

For us eighth graders, the poetry was "kid stuff," until one sneaky girl in our class cozied up to our "idol" and slyly asked, "Teacher, will you write one little poem for me, please?" and then handed him her album.

"Oh, how childish," we said.

Envying her guts, it did not take long before our poetry albums were popular again. We would not let her get away with it. Mr. Long Legs happily collected our albums with a charming smile and we were thrilled. We huddled with the lucky one in the corner of the playground and interpreted his lovely rhyme, making much more of it than was said.

Because I was afraid he did not like me very much, I waited and then finally with some courage, laid my album on his desk. Not daring to ask him to return it, I worried, "Could my album be lost?"

When he finally came to me, I shivered, feeling his hand ever so slightly stroking my blond hair. He playfully pulled on one of my thick braids.

Blushing, I heard one of my friends giggling behind me, but were they jealous when they read the caption.

"To: My Wild Song Bird."

His wish for me was short and very solemn, rather disappointing, I thought.

> *May God lead you in green meadows,*
> *Where his little lambs do feed.*
> *Do not listen to the lying spirit*
> *of the evil whispering of deceit.*

He had pasted a beautiful picture of a green vase filled with purple violets and lilies of the valleys on the left page. It was a little heart of pink rosebuds with his P.S. that made all my friends green with envy. I read, "Please don't ever forget your Mister L.L.!"

No, I would never, not ever.

I kept it a secret from my parents, especially my mother.

In a small town, there are very few secrets. Casually, Mother asked, "Did you, like the other girls, receive a nice poem from the new teacher?" She demanded to read it.

I expected she would put a

damper on my romance. Reading my special P.S., her reaction clobbered my budding love.

"You are not any more important than your friends!" To emphasize her concern, she said, "Three girls in town have been wearing the same necklace. Who knows how many he gave a necklace to before he came here? You are old enough to be wiser."

Mister L. L. may have been a Romeo but for me the eighth grade was no waste. After many decades, one glance at that little heart made of rosebuds makes me feel like a favorite and very special.

Mr. L. L. did not teach the next eighth grade at our school. He made too many girls feel "Special". Our hero went to look for lambs in greener meadows.

I have lost my diploma for successfully completing eight years of grade school, but have saved my report booklet. On the page with sixth grade marking periods is a tear stain. It happened when I received a six for Math. My parents would only accept an eight and above. Mem was very angry. Her dark brown eyes flashed. "You can do better!" she said. I heard that often during my school days. I was a girl, why should I try?

Willemke our maid got married. Not having to pay her wages helped my parents save for my brother's education. Mother needed me. Our parents valued education and compromised. I was enrolled in a Home Education-Agriculture school halftime. That meant on Monday and Friday I biked through wind and weather, twenty K.M. to a girl's school where I learned cooking, sewing and the basics of housekeeping.

I hated every minute of it, except for one course, a class on gardening and tending to small animals. I learned how to set a broody hen on eggs. This was all we learned about agriculture. We could have learned it all at home, except that it would have been even more boring.

At the end of three years, our mothers attended a show to see what we had accomplished. Displayed between fancy dresses, neatly sewn aprons, knitted woolen jerseys were small squares of white and pink cotton with perfectly hand-made buttonholes, six in a row. Mother was impressed that so many had my name. She proudly approached the teacher, remarking what nice work I had done.

"Yes, those were made by Amy," the prudish old maid teacher said. "I am sorry there was a need to discipline her so often for being inattentive."

The buttonholes did not make it home. My diploma says, "Graduating with 'average' results." We were graded, "excellent, very good, good, and the other."

The outdoors was where I came alive and I shared that love for nature with my Father. Together we roamed the fields and explored the best fishing holes.

Although my breasts tried to develop under layers of clothing, no boy noticed it. Mother hoping for nature to do a miracle, forced the process with spoons full of cod liver oil and rendered suet, the tallow sticking to my teeth on the way to school.

Skinny and tall, my legs had little attraction and I refused to "put up" my hair like the other girls my age. One boy pulled on those long braids and teasingly asked, "Are you still in grade school, Amy?" Twisting my braids, he hoped to sneak a kiss. I was furious, but liked it. So trying to make peace, he bought the most expensive candy, called "Owl skins," for the slips of paper inside that wrapper predicted the future, much like the fortune cookies of today.

"I like you," he said and tried to kiss me again, receiving a slap in his face.

It was on an Ascension Day, at an outdoor concert where my parents met that I nearly danced beside him to the rhythm of the band music.

John Boersma was not in our "class." His family was poor and they lived simple lives, having only the bare necessities for their many children.

Afraid my parents would not approve, I told him, "You must leave me near the old church."

Coming home alone, the door was locked and knocking several times, I found that all doors were locked! I pleaded at the window nearest to the bed closet where my parents slept, and finally my father opened the front door. "Mem is very upset; you will have to explain why you were with John Boersma all day," he said.

From the tone of his voice I knew he was not angry with me but more worried about my mother. Standing in front of the bed closet, I told her, "I am home now." She turned her face to the wall, rejecting a possible apology.

"Go to bed!" she said. She probably did not want me to see her tears.

"Don't tell Mem. One of her best friends noticed you with John. She humiliated your mother saying, 'Can't your Amy find a boy other than one of the Boersma family?' " Everyone at the neighbor's birthday party had heard the news.

"Yemerke." I knew he cared when my father used my nickname. "Will you promise Mem never to see John again?" It hurt to see my father beg me. For his sake I promised never to meet John again, but I vowed to leave home at the best opportunity. I would see the world, the places where I had read about, Indonesia with its islands and wild forest and the many other Dutch colonies too, different places and adventure anywhere!

Mother made an appointment for my hair to be cut. "Nice boys don't want a girl with braids." She added sternly, "It's time to grow up!"

But I cried myself to sleep, the stubby hair irritating my neck. During the day, it kept escaping from a wire that was supposed to shape my locks. My impossible unruly mop was a constant reminder of what I was not.

That summer mother suggested that on weekends I should visit my cousins in Friesland who were a year older and flirted. I was miserable. It had been fun with John.

At home, everyone called on me. Father needed me in the bakery, Mother in the store or in the house. "You are the older one and you should be wiser." I heard it too often. Sometimes she compared me with Beppe Hoekstra, having no heart, cold and tough.

Mem had a great loving heart although I could not see it. Her large kettle of soup that she cooked on Friday was a burden to me. When I rode my bike home from school, I could already smell the soup at the neighbor's house.

A huge soup bone had simmered for hours and then she added rice to the broth. Greens of the "Soup plant", a celeriac supposedly gave it flavor. In the summer the plant thrived in our garden. It survived in the winter. At last, one pound of lean ground beef, rolled into small meatballs completed the brew. Then it was a thick soup that stuck to our ribs. A dessert of cream-of-wheat with dried prunes stretched the meal for possible guests.

One guest might be old Mr. Post who came clip-clopping in his wooden shoes to our home, carrying his shiny spade on his shoulder. He was too old for heavy farm work and no use to the man he had served faithfully. With his wife now sickly, they had rented a small house in town. By noon he had spaded half of our garden into neat raised beds, one perfectly measured slice of rich dirt after another. I admired the little wiry man. "Hi Amy," he'd say placing himself next to my father at the table. Mister Post was an elder in the church and my father only a deacon, so he would politely ask Mister Post to return thanks for the food, but he was served last for he was our hired man.

A guest also might be a salesman of a large firm or a widow who helped Mother with the heavy work on Friday. She served the businessman before my father and didn't ask him to pray. I thought it odd, but Heit said, "I don't know if he goes to 'our church'!"

All of the family would lick their spoons and scrape the last gooey thick soup from their plates, except me. It was a giant undertaking to empty my bowl with Mother having no mercy. "Amy, you know there are people living right here in this town who would smack their lips to have a taste of my soup," she would say.

Yes, and I knew who they were, but that thick rice soup refused to go down. Besides, that soup on Saturday was still my responsibility.

The left-over soup thickened overnight. Adding a little water and a pinch of salt, Mother had her soup ready to distribute to those families who she knew would not only smack their lips but needed nourishment.

Under the cover of darkness, I first brought a container to old Mister Post and his ailing wife. "Now remember, Amy, you don't stop to talk with anyone. Go straight to his back door and quietly slip it inside. Should he call, don't answer him, but leave immediately."

Carefully following her instruction, I hurried home. There were more deliveries to make. A young couple had drifted in a makeshift houseboat down a canal and moored their drafty shelter to a willow tree in a draining ditch. By accident, my father had found them on his delivery route, far enough removed from people to be discovered and fined for trespassing.

"The man is gone for days, leaving the woman alone with her baby," he told mother.

She did not need more information. The pan of soup had no bottom, and by Saturday night, she stacked day-old bread in the basement to give away.

Tramping through the soggy fields, I plodded past the dark silhouettes of drowsy cows to the folks in the houseboat. "You may not embarrass them. Drop it off at the end of the gang plank," my mother said.

She may not have thought the transients might have been fugitives, or did she? Running home as if the evil one was behind me, I got only a glimpse of our cozy living room and everyone reading their favorite magazine. We exchanged weekly and monthly periodicals with friends from church. That they weren't up to date made little difference. They were an interesting and economical arrangement during the depression.

The last secret and most difficult mission was to a poor family on Mill Street. Muddy and dark, the deep ruts in that two track were to be avoided. The slimy slush would stick to my wooden shoes, and I could lose one easily on the spooky road.

Sometimes, against mother's warning, I went inside that house and looked at poverty that was beyond my understanding. The one room was heated by a small stove that burned peat dug from an area that contained sulfuric acid. It had a horrible smell. A baby slept in a box close to the stove near his father who coughed constantly. Another child played in a small bed closet where the potatoes also were stored. Diapers drying on a makeshift line near the ceiling hadn't been washed properly; the stench of urine added to all the misery of that family.

Mother had good reasons to keep me from visiting with the woman who invited me in because she was so pitifully lonely. Her husband was probably in the advanced state of tuberculosis.

I often asked myself why I had to do this. None of my friends went on soup routes and certainly not my brother, now reading the good stories in the weekly portfolio.

Stumbling and groping in the dark on a rainy cold night, I thought I had bumped into the ghost of Vrouwe Snackenburg and screamed.

She answered, "You hit me!"

"No! No! I did not, Who are you?" I felt a slimy horribly messy junk dripping on my coat.

"Oh Yuck!" I shivered. "Go away!"

"Amy, is that you?" I heard a familiar voice now. "When you hit me, you broke those eggs."

Recognizing my best friend Deeny, I shouted, "No, you ran into me. What are you doing here?"

"Mother sends me every week after dark with a couple dozen cracked eggs. I hate this job," my friend said.

"I have to take soup and old bread."

"Well, they won't have scrambled eggs this week," Deeny said.

Blaming our mothers, we walked home, keeping the disaster a secret. Was this not our secret mission? It had to be!

I still feel a twinge of guilt when I re-

Fourteen After a Soup Run in Wooden Shoes

fuse a good bowl of soup by saying, "I don't care much for soup!" And I remember my mother teaching her unwilling daughter that rice soup is to be given to a person who needs to know someone cares.

Leaving

*T*he blue granite stairs to the solid double doors of the main building were worn from many feet, heavy with their own burden. Many had pulled on the copper handle as I did on a day in August, 1939, and I was scared. When I heard the noise of footsteps on the white marble vestibule floor, my heart jumped crazily when a middle aged lady dressed in a navy blue uniform asked,"Who is it you would like to see?"

"May I speak to the director of nurses?" I said.

"Do you have an appointment?"

I shook my head, fearing the chance for a new adventure might turn into defeat. I told her, "Please, those who brought me are waiting. I live in another province."

"Follow me, I'll ask Sister DeVries if she will see you," she said.

Vacationing with my Uncle in Friesland, we were on a boat trip to Leeuwarden, mooring across from the Diaconessen Hospital. A girl may have a chance to apply for a free education in a nursing course by working hard.

My relatives planned to visit a museum and the old church where the princes of the House of Orange were buried, but I decided to begin a new life and now stood in front of a huge oak desk facing a stern woman. Her cold, clear blue eyes captured me, and puckering her full lips, she observed me from head to toe.

Then she asked, "So, why are you here?"

I knew immediately we would have many confrontations, but explained that I wanted an education.

"You have no higher education?" Staring me down, she remarked, "Tseck, tseck. So and you would like to be a nurse?"

"Yes, that is why I am here," I said.

"We'll have to see if you have potential. So you are not quite eighteen? For the first year you must wash dishes, maybe

75

longer. Would you like to fill out an application?"

She handed me a sheet. When I took it, she said, "Remember, keep your nails very short and clean."

Answering the questions in the form quickly, I signed it nervously, "Y. Hoekstra."

The same lady escorted me to the door again. Somewhat amused, she asked," Well?"

"I've applied for the nursing program," I said.

"By taking a short cut. I hope to see you again," she said.

Six months later a letter of acceptance arrived. My parents might have been surprised or maybe relieved. Father was secretly proud of me and gave me a loan for the uniforms I needed when my total savings of about one hundred and fifty guilders did not cover the expenses.

Mother and I went shopping and it was a day of warm communication and understanding, one of the best memories I have of her.

With the six gray uniforms, twelve white aprons, and three nurses caps, I would look like a nurse. Washing dishes, hundreds of dishes, pots and pans every day would prove that I had potential.

The day we shopped in Leeuwarden, Mother wanted to meet the director of nurses and insisted she see Sister DeVries. Returning shortly, her eyes were dark with a spark of fire. She was tightlipped and very quiet. I knew the meeting was not cordial, and I admired her courage.

On March 15th, a few weeks before the world blew up in the second world war, I left our village of Lutjegast. Mother took my face in both her hands and said, "Oh Amy, you are so young!"

I knew she wished we had been closer and I had the same feeling.

The same lady I had met before greeted me at the hospital and showed me my dorm room. She asked, "Do you speak Dutch, Groningen dialect, or Frisian?"

"All three," I said, very emphatically. Was this person testing my intelligence?

She laughed and spoke Frisian now, and she chuckled and laughed louder when we unpacked my suitcases filled with warm woolen underwear.

"Mem wanted you to be warm," she said and smiling, gave me one of the new pink jerseys. "Why don't you change now? I'll store these heavy things in a spare closet."

She was frank and forward and I liked her. The stiff starched collars on my uniform chafed my neck. My cap tried to slip on one ear but I was proud, feeling liberated.

For the time being, I washed stacks of dishes with the initials D.H. and was very homesick.

Every two weeks I had a weekend off and lost so much weight that Mother told me it would be all right for me to return home. Stubbornly riding my bike the thirty KM to the hospital, I was proving that I had potential for the nursing profession. My Dad rode beside me part of the way, or I probably would have quit. We did not talk much. He was tired from a long and hard day of work and it was enough that he cared. Always parting at the same corner of the highway, he would wave, raising his arm in a grand gesture above his head.

In the second week of May, Hitler's army conquered the Lowlands, bombing cities and dikes and inundating our fertile country with salty water of the North Sea. They needed me and transferred me to the surgical floor where the dying and wounded patients lay in rows of makeshift beds, and I began the very disciplined training of a first year nurse.

First Year of War, First Year Nurse

The prospect of sitting for hours at the bedside of a dying patient was part of training for a future nurse, probably a disciplinary testing for composure in the face of death. I dreaded the hours spent in the makeshift isolated corner in the instrument room. Hope for recovery, restoration of life, health and happiness was my idealistic goal for the nursing profession.

The man would die where two sterilizers puffed steam, rubber tubes dangled from the ceiling, tables and carts set with instruments and bandages, and an inexperienced nurse waited until he was almost drawing his last breath. Only then would I ask for the head nurse. If I called her too early, she'd tell me, "Sister Hoekstra, we are busy." If the warning came too late, I received the blame.

Medical technology, primitive as it was, did not insure our patients an easy death, and it was wartime. Pain killers and anesthetics were scarce or not even available. We washed bandages and used them again and again. Penicillin had not been invented. Yesterday I had watched a woman die for lack of sulfa tablets.

The darkened room was depressingly somber, and with the man's pulse becoming irregular, I rationalized, "Nobody, actually not a doctor or nurse, has any influence on healing. In the medical field all that is left is assisting death, and it is a miracle when someone survives surgery."

Earlier that morning, the doctor who was forced to perform a D and C without an anesthetic had nervously tried to calm his patient. "Let go of the nurse, lady," he said. She screamed, grabbing me hard and we restrained her. Hoping to give her assurance, my hand rested on her shoulder. I was cringing myself when I heard the scraping of the instruments inside her womb. Being a woman, I abhorred the procedure.

I touched the comatose man's nose and it was very cold. Applying a mixture of glycerine and lemon to his parched tongue with a little brush, I waited and rolled more bandages. The hours ticked slowly on the wooden oak clock. For me the world stood still, a dark stagnant pool of decay. A robin chirped, concerned for her young in a nest on the ivy covering the hospital wall, it sounded shrill, artificial and unreal.

The head nurse came. I thought to check on my patient. Surprisingly, I heard her say, "Sister Hoekstra, a man is on the phone. He tells me he wants to speak to you. I told him personal phone calls cannot be accepted. He persisted, saying it has to do with his sister who is sick."

She took my place at the bedside, very annoyed at the necessity of covering for a student nurse.

Puzzled, I thought, Who can this be?

"This is sister Hoekstra speaking," I said.

"Oh, Amy, I got through to you. Do you have a few hours off Saturday afternoon? My sister has a bad cold and I have an

Sisters Comparing Notes

extra ticket to an organ concert in the Grote Kerk."

"Your sister?" I had not quite come back to the world of the living yet.

"Yes, my sister Leatitia Van Ooyen. She took you to our home one day. I am her brother, Claude."

"Oh," I said, remembering he was working in the central building of the Telephone Company.

"No, it is impossible. I have the weekend off and will take the train at four thirty for home."

This was unexpected and I didn't give him a chance.

"Too bad," he said, clearly

79

disappointed.

"Maybe next week," I managed to say, but I heard the phone click.

"The man was telling me his sister is sick," I explained to the irritated nurse.

Very few men were willing to go out with a nurse who dressed in a uniform that resembled a devout nun. What had I told him? How stupid of me. I could have taken the later train. Worrying all weekend, the days at home dragged on. Anxious and wondering if he might call again, I was glad to return to my work and pleased to see that I had the night duty for the next two weeks. Night duty gave us extra time off. And during the day sirens did not scream, calling us to the floor. It was later in the evening when the Allied forces flew to the industrial Rhur area in Germany, the German Luftwaffe retaliating with all hell breaking loose above the North Sea.

By Friday I had almost lost all hope that Claude would call me again. Making my evening rounds along the rows of patients, I checked them by the pale glimmer of my flashlight covered by blue tissue paper. To confuse Hitler's enemies, the country was in total darkness, and the command was strictly enforced by our German oppressors.

Reporting back at the station, I heard my superior answer the phone. "It is for you, Amy," she said.

"Is it possible to make yourself free for a few hours tomorrow?" Claude asked.

"Yes, I'm on night duty now," I said, hoping he didn't hear the excitement in my voice.

"I'll wait at the gate at two o'clock. There is another organ concert in the Grote Kerk," he said and hung up.

"A social call?" my colleague asked.

"Yes, I've a date tomorrow afternoon. Please keep it a secret."

"How did he get past the switchboard?" she asked.

"I don't know, but he works for the telephone company," I told her.

Later that night we heard the planes droning across the

North Sea and the sirens sounding an alarm. Our hospital, having a contract to assist in unusual circumstances at residences in the area, sometimes received a call for help at night.

"Sister Hoekstra, someone died. They've asked for a nurse who will prepare him for burial. Tonight it's your turn," the person at the switchboard said.

"I have not done this. Can't it be postponed?"

The thought of going out in the pitch dark with sirens screaming and beams of lights above the North Sea searching for enemy planes was frightening. There was enemy fire or even "the Allies" dropping their deadly load trying to escape for home base.

"You've had plenty of experience lately. Don't you know what it means? The man is dead!" And she was not finished yet. "Sister Hoekstra, you will not receive any more calls. This is a hospital, not a dating service!"

Wrapping myself in a black woolen cape made me feel more dismal and gloomy than the world outside. I grabbed a flash-light and disappeared into the dark.

The night watchman, opening the creaky iron gate said, "Dark night, sister." Then recognizing me he said, "Be careful Amy! Things get worse daily. Heard tonight on the radio that Hitler gave an order, all public meeting places and churches too will be closed."

"Closed? Churches too?"

"Yes, don't worry. A nurse is quite safe." The good-hearted man, sensing my apprehension, wished me once more a good night.

By the shaded light of my flashlight, I found the address on Transvaal street and as if they had been watching from inside at number eleven, the front door opened at my arrival.

Two tiny women confronted me, "Sister, sister, we don't know what to do."

Sick about war, its restrictions, and sure that Claude knew there was no concert, I was now facing a dead man. The women chattered in unison, and I was a frightened young girl following them to the living room where, on a day bed, the dead man lay.

I noticed his fine features, a neatly trimmed goatee and a

kind expression on his face. I asked the women to leave the room. Now alone with the dead man, I lost all fear and we communicated, if not physically. He wore many layers of clothing and I undressed him to his last neat linen shirt, lifting him carefully on a large coffee table. Then I changed the bedding, which laid with his "death shirt" folded on a chair. Finally, he rested on the clean sheets, wearing a traditional white burial shirt with a little black bow at his neck.

I imagined him saying, "Thank you sister," and I scared myself, actually answering, "It is a privilege, sir." It didn't seem right to pull the sheet over the man's face and I folded it lightly over his hands. He looked satisfied and peaceful. I then told the women my work was finished and I must leave for my work at the hospital.

"No, no, Sister, you must stay. We made real coffee. We've hoarded it for months. It's for special occasions. You cannot leave us now."

To refuse their hospitality would be almost rude. They offered me a slice of candied honey cake and talked, telling me in detail their problems and anxiety now they were left to cope. "He was so kind Sister. We three were very close." I learned they were sisters-in-law.

I was about to leave when one woman asked. "Sister, did you remove my husband's wedding ring?"

I had not! The thought of having to again go in that room terrified me and a chill creeping up my spine made me feel sick.

"Sister, please?" the woman begged.

The work wasn't finished. His fingers now were stiffening when I pried the wedding ring off his finger. It was then that I realized this was the end of this man's life, the very end! I threw the ring on the dining room table at the sobbing woman, grabbed the black cape, and fled into the darkness of the night.

The sirens screamed again and the sinister noise vibrated with my fear of death and dying. I kept on running as if bewitched, the black cape flapping from my shoulders.

At the mailbox on a corner near the hospital, I stumbled over the legs of a soldier passionately making love with his girl.

Startled at what he perceived a ghost, he swore, "My Gott! Heil Hitler!"

Recovering quickly, I heard him hollering, "Du Swheinhund!"

Exhausted, leaning against the fence and waiting for the porter to open the gate, I vomited violently, retching against an insane world.

They hardly noticed when I returned to the floor. It was almost daybreak, and patients were wakened. We had to make reports. By six thirty, the day shift came. At seven, the head nurse summoned me to her office to tell me it had to be absolutely my last phone call from the outside.

Discouraged and tired, I went up to my room. Sure that the organ concert was canceled, Claude probably was not waiting for me.

By two o'clock, rested and curious, I looked from the window of the dormitory hall and noticed him pacing back and forth at the gate.

"You are late," he said, when I, out of breath, met him. I was not sure he was relieved to see me or disappointed by my tardiness. Trying to match his long strides, I thought there seemed to be no reason for an excuse.

As the cold northwest wind blew a drizzly rain in our faces, we crossed the bridge over the canal that once was a moat protecting the residence of Prince Willem the Orange. Then we followed a cobble stone alley that led to the Grote Kerk where the former royal family had worshipped.

Nailed to the heavy plated door was, as I had expected, Hitler's decree. "BY ORDER OF THE FURHER THE CHURCH IS CLOSED FOR PUBLIC MEETINGS UNTIL FURTHER NOTICE."

"Nasty Moffen," Claude scolded, pretending that he was unaware of the new rule.

"Too bad," I said as if I was also surprised.

"Well, we could take a nice walk. I know a small trail along a dike." He looked at me as if questioning my fitness.

"Okay," I told him, not very enthusiastic about the prospect of getting drenched. Now it rained steadily with no shelter from the driving northwest wind on the dike.

Here and there a few sheep huddled, finding rescue from the inundated meadows. Claude didn't talk much, and needing all my breath to keep up with him, I followed. We made it back to the hospital gate in record time.

"How about going to church with me? What are your hours tomorrow?" he asked.

Weary and cold, I told him, "During the day we need our sleep. The late service is better for me."

Before three, he was promptly at the gate and we hurried to church. He was about a step ahead of me at the Pelican Church where the nurses occupied a reserved pew. Claude shoved next to me as if he was one of us. He looked up the hymns for me as we sang together from his book. I was pleased that my colleagues noticed his courteous manner. At the end of the service, we shuffled to the foyer, listening to the organ play a joyful postlude. Suddenly Claude stopped at the back of the sanctuary and listened until the last note of music faded. Then, taking my arm, he said, "That was good, Amy. I would like you to meet my Mother."

Several times his sister had taken me home and I knew his mother quite well, but this time Claude introduced me officially and said, "This is Amy and I'm going to marry her someday."

I wasn't at all so sure! But his mother insisted we should drink a Sunday afternoon cup of tea.

The following Sunday, German soldiers were stationed at all church services and all public meetings. By Saturday the Grote Kerk again was opened for afternoon organ concerts. I now gladly accepted Claude's invitation, hoping for an afternoon of happy music and fun, a real relief from the hospital routine.

I began to have second thoughts when we entered the church vestibule, our footsteps resounding hollow on the black granite floor. We passed the white marble statues of Prince Willem the Orange and his entire family posing on their decorative graves. For centuries, they'd been staring blindly from behind iron bars at us, the people coming and leaving the sanctuary. Locked in death, the solemn group looked desperate in their confinement.

I shivered. Groups of music-loving listeners sat scattered in the unheated pews of the old cathedral. The cold dampened church was depressingly quiet until, suddenly and loudly, Bach's deep organ tones thundered through the sanctuary, engulfing the huge pillars and rolling up to the rafters. I wanted to hide, cover my ears and crawl under the pew, escaping all the overpowering noise.

I was cold and looked at Claude, envying his warm woolen coat. Hoping to find a little comfort, I shoved closer to him, but he was totally absorbed by Bach's music and paid no attention to me. He politely moved over, leaving me with more room to shiver. I watched his serious face and decided, "This man is too old for me!"

Finally, the concert ended, and chilled to the bone, we slowly walked with the meager audience to the hall, again passing the elaborate statues. I nodded them a solemn farewell.

"Isn't Bach's music magnificent? His compositions are like a beautiful woven tapestry in warm colors, " Claude said.

Hmmm! I thought and then realized that there was much to learn about Bach and the serious young man who loved his music. I never expected that someday I would be his wife and there would be many organ concerts to follow.

Second Year Nurse

O ur small room on the fourth floor of the administration building had little ventilation, except for a skylight giving us a glimmer of daylight. They assigned us first year students to a little nook commonly known as the chicken loft.

My friend Dove and I had frequently applied for housing in the dorm for second year students. It fell on deaf ears. We were appointed to be "big sisters" to new girls who came to the city, a questionable honor. Once they were used to institutional life and beginning to feel at home, they moved to another apartment and assigned to us another homesick girl. In the summer we sweltered. On rainy days, the stuffy place smelled filthy.

When Marie and Jean were introduced to us, we knew that this time it would be a real challenge. Not only did we have to teach them the hospital routine and keep them reasonably happy, we needed to give them basic lessons in personal hygiene also. After living in the country deprived of modern conveniences, showers frightened Marie. Ours was the old- fashioned type. We had to light a gas heater before turning the faucets on. Undressed and in tears, Marie fled to our room. "That thing goes Phuff!" she said.

Still crying and sniffling, we watched her slip a new flannel nightgown over her head and crawl into bed, no doubt forlorn and homesick.

Jeany, worried now, also began to undress and remove her shoes. Her perspiring feet gave off a horrible odor. Dove, my friend, as gentle as her name, yelled, "Phew" and dumped her shoes out in the hallway.

"We'll have to teach you girls a few things," she said. "Amy, will you take Phuff to the shower and you, Phew, come with me."

The girls caught on quickly, but a distinct odor constantly

reminded us of Phew's problem with stinky feet.

On a particularly hot day, hoping to find relief and a breath of fresh air, I pulled myself up through the skylight and slid on the roof tiles to a wide gutter that connected with the hospital building. I had planned to study with a beautiful view over the city. Across from me was one window of the hospital floor.

Someone knocking on that window interrupted me and I recognized our director of nurses, Ma de Vries. Very agitated, she motioned to me. No doubt she wasn't very pleased with a nurse positioned high on a roof. I squeaked again through the small window, and she was waiting for me before my dangling feet found the chair in the center of our room.

"Sister Hoekstra," she said. "Was this your idea for sun tanning?" Her cold blue eyes stared me down sarcastically. "This is awful, a sister of Diaconessen Hospital sitting on the roof."

I had no excuse for my behavior other than the smelly dark room.

"What do I smell here?" she said. Sniffing and snorting, Ma de Vries tried to find the origin of the odor. Searching under all four beds, she pulled out a pair of shoes. "Phew!" she said. "Do these shoes belong to you?"

"No, Sister de Vries, they belong to our new roommate. We nicknamed her Phew," I said.

Closet inspection was a regular routine for our dorm house-keeper, but Ma opened our closet door with four laundry bags and detected the smell again. She held her nose and asked, "Sister Hoekstra, what were you doing on that roof?"

"I was trying to study, hoping to find a breath of fresh air, sister."

She didn't think it very amusing. Her blue eyes blinked at a puny sun ray peeking through the skylight. Surprising me she asked, "Are you and Sister Nieuwenhuis second year nurses now? This room is too crowded for four beds, but large enough for the two new girls."

I nodded smugly, hoping the acrobatic experience on the roof was a timely exercise.

"In the house of Sister Keuning is a room available for two.

It's on the third floor. She is very old and I trust you will behave according to the hospital rules. No noise after eleven p.m. That is curfew and men are not allowed to visit. No entertaining of any kind or you have to ask for permission."

"Oh yes," I said. Knowing Sister Keuning was very hard of hearing and also kind, we would have no problem.

"How did you do it? Did you go to Ma de Vries?" my friend asked.

"No, Ma came here. She got me off the roof," I said.

Dove always had a great sense of humor. This time she acted as if it was normal to sit on the roof. After returning from night shift, she had most of our moving finished and we had finally graduated to the second year nurses' quarters. We stayed there through the third year too.

Our boyfriends, Claude and Frans, were not too shy to climb the three long stairways to our room. Probably Sister Keuning, well aware of their trespassing in the world of women, kindly remembered her youth and I rewarded her frequently with a fresh honey cake when I returned from weekends at home. The luxury of sweet baked goods had become scarce in the crowded cities during the war.

We had a good warning system for Ma de Vries inspections, and it worked perfectly when Tjits Hoogsteen was present. She had a small reed organ and, at the sight of Ma, began playing hymns accompanying her falsetto soprano at the top of her lungs. Ma left very pleased by our choice of entertainment until once Claude and Frans were almost caught. We had told them not to speak on the stairs. A man's voice sounded like a rooster's crow in a flock of hens. They were usually good, but when we blew them a kiss one night on the top of the stairwell, they hollered, "Good night, we'll be back soon."

A door opened when they fled outside and Ma climbed the stairs. Lights were out and she found us sleeping soundly. We heard her ask our musician, "Were there men here?"

Romance was never a part of Ma de Vries' life, and she tried to snuff it out at the first opportunity. For weeks we were a target for her nightly exercises. One night when the organ played,

Claude and Frans were with us. They escaped to a walk-in closet and we hid them between our clothes. It took a long time before we felt the coast was clear. The hours spent in the stuffy closet were a true test of love, we thought.

But the huge red cross painted on the roof did not guarantee safety against the shelling and bombing of the city. When the sirens blared, we had to dress fully and return to our station on the floor. At night we fell asleep to the drone of war planes flying to Germany along the North Sea boundaries. Early in the morning they returned, sometimes followed by German Luftwaffe. The Allied forces as well as the enemy dropped their deadly cargo wherever, in the ocean or on land.

At night, they turned our power off by eleven p.m. Dressing by a dim flashlight, at the first scream of sirens, brought my friend into a comical situation. She sat on her bed kicking at a shoe. When I returned from a scene with a patient whose family experienced a direct hit by a bomb, I asked, "Something wrong?"

She gave her shoe another kick and it flew under my bed. "How's your patient?" she asked.

"I'll tell you later. Where have you been?"

"On the floor with an old man. He's dead. When I brought him to the morgue, I met with Ma de Vries." Fighting her tears, her nurse's cap sagged sadly on her blond curls over one ear. "That woman," she said. "She stopped me and asked in her sweetest voice, 'Sister Nieuwenhuis, why do you wear two shoes of a different color? My nurses are to dress properly at all times.'"

I looked at the black shoe on her foot, the brown one was under my bed, and I began to laugh. But then Dove said, "When Ma told me not to laugh, I gave her a piece of my mind and said, 'You are the most picky and cold person I ever met. People are dying. The world is in a mess! I hate your sick attitude and...' "

"What?" I asked, knowing my friend could be blunt.

"I have to see Doctor Kruik, Pa, the director of the hospital this afternoon at two o'clock. Not for the dress code but for shooting off my mouth."

"He will understand. I know he will. He has an anatomy class at two this afternoon."

"No, there will be an autopsy and you have to be present also."

"I've had a rough night too. The family I brought in all had serious shrapnel wounds. The woman lay on a stretcher and kept asking 'How is my family?' I told her everyone was living and well taken care of. When the surgeon came to check on her, he asked me to assist him saying, 'Sister, leave the tourniquet and carefully hold up her leg.' When he cut her heavy wool stocking, I held the bloody limb. It was completely severed. I have never known that one leg is so heavy and I almost dropped it.

Swearing under his breath, the surgeon had said, 'Damned War! Give her a megadose of morphine sister!' I stayed with her until she went to surgery.

Then he reminded me to be at anatomy by two this afternoon."

Dove said, "No, it's changed. Don't forget. You need to be at the autopsy for my patient." She left for day shift and I, just returning from night shift, went to bed for a few hours' sleep.

Not all the sirens in the world could have awakened me until Dove shook me and shouted, "Amy, wake up! You missed the two o'clock anatomy." She waved a note from Pa Kruik in my face. He and the surgeon were friends." He said he reminded you on the floor. He thought you were delayed. Where have you been? It is after four now."

"Here. How did your appointment with Pa go?"

"All he said was a nurse may never lose her temper and I have to apologize to Sister de Vries. He then smiled and told me to remember to wear two black shoes.

In spite of everything, I laughed out loud and asked, "Was everyone present?"

"Yes, we were. It was a very old person. The surgeon told us, 'The autopsy was valuable because the body had already been deteriorating from disease, old age and malnutrition, even though he was a victim of war.'"

Checking my patients during the night shift, I came across the woman who had lost her leg. She was glad to see me and, smiling now, talked about the ordeal. "Thank you, Sister," she said. "I only lost my leg and the doctor promised to give me a new limb. Our neighbor lost his life!" Holding her hand, I thought she almost wished to comfort me.

By 9 o'clock the next morning, I stood wearing a fresh cap and clean starched white apron, shaking in shiny black shoes in front of Pa Kruik's office door.

I heard his deep voice say, "Yes!" He sat behind his large oak desk and motioned for me to sit down. He was an enormous person with thick silver gray hair combed back. Taking off his glasses, he looked straight at me.

"Sister Hoekstra, do you have an explanation why you were absent at the autopsy? Had not Doctor Straat asked for your assistance?"

"Yes Sir," It was ridiculous to tell him I had overslept, impossibly stupid.

"Did you forget, Sister?"

"No, Doctor." I then whispered, "I overslept sir."

"That is inexcusable, Sister Hoekstra. This semester I will have to give you a failing grade for anatomy."

"Please, Doctor, I'm sorry."

About in tears, I was going to leave when I heard him say, "Sister Hoekstra, I myself will perform the next autopsy. I expect you to assist me. Understand?"

"Yes, Doctor, I will be present. Thank you, Sir."

Doctor Kruik performed the next autopsy on a pregnant young woman. A German police officer had found her body in an alley and brought it to the morgue. A possible illegal abortion, the doctor told us. Lecturing us first on the sanctity of life, he then told me to stand near him with the officer who was also present.

Doctor Kruik, cold and correct in a professional manner, revealed the perfectly healthy organs of a human being, explaining their functions. Then when exposing the uterus, he hesitated, and before he removed the four month old fetus, I heard him whisper, "Too bad!"

"Well, sisters," he said. "You learned today that the body functions perfectly unless men interfere. This young male could have been a fine soldier for Mein Fuhrer." His sarcasm cut sharper than the knife in his hand.

"Heil Hitler!" The officer saluted in protest. Remembering the German soldier passionately making love at the mailbox in front of the gate one night, I again felt like I would vomit. Fiercely rebelling, I said, "Swheinhund!"

The word reverberated in the morgue.

"Sister Hoekstra, you are immediately dismissed from this class," I heard Pa Kruik say.

Slamming shut the heavy iron door, I was numb and leaned my head against the cold wall of the morgue until all my classmates had left.

At last Doctor Kruik came. He gave me the tray with the fetus. "Deliver this to the lab, Sister Hoekstra. For assisting me today, you pass anatomy with an A. I tell you so now, before the German police arrest me."

The final passing grade was insignificant compared to the intense feeling of holding the perfectly formed human fetus. His head was so large for its small body and perhaps contained a wisdom far beyond my hate and confusion. Could he have been conceived of love in a war torn world of hate?

June 29, 1944

I n the midst of our U.P. winter, 1997, I took the time to go through some boxes stored in the attic. There, under the eaves, I found many memories of our married life. Reading through the old clippings, home-made cards from the children, and letters written by our parents in Holland, I realized what a busy time that must have been. A half century of sadness, joy, triumphs, failures and much humor too, were pressed and bundled in a worn carton box.

The love notes of our children, some telling us about their frustrations, now made me laugh. I read them to Claude and he snickered too. I knew he was perfectly happy and content living our quiet life in the forest, but I wished those years had not passed so quickly.

I dug deeper into the hidden corners for the old books stored there, again a reminder of change and former roots. Written in Dutch and Frisian language, those books were old acquaintances but almost foreign. I wondered, "Am I a stranger? Where do I belong?"

My knees began to hurt from kneeling on the hard floor, and changing to a more comfortable position, I began to compare and read the text from a very old Bible, comparing it to the English version. Turning to the title page, I was surprised to find my married name written in beautiful calligraphy, YMKJE VAN OOYEN. It was the name of the grandma I was named for, who married ROEL VANDERWAL. This was their wedding bible. Oddly, I have no recollection of who gave it to me. I read, "In Memory of your marriage, 1882. I Cor. 14:13 by your friend, J.N.W. Plet." The Bible was printed by the British Bible Society in the year MDCXVIII.

Looking up their wedding text, I was puzzled about the meaning of that verse for my grandparents that day. "For anyone who speaks in a strange tongue should pray that he may interpret what He says." I Cor. 13:13 seemed to be much more appropriate, "Now these three remain, Faith, Hope and Love. But the greatest of these is Love." Yet, today, a fine purple cutout for a bookmark is still on that page of the text.

I found our wedding Bible too, tattered with a broken spine, it was a newer edition of the same size, also with a plain black cover. My Father wrote, "VAN UW OUDERS, by UW Huweyk 6-29-1944. Text EFEZE 5:32." Our names were omitted, and as in my grandparent's Bible, the exact date had not been recorded. Someday our children may have questions about our text. "This is a mystery, but I speak of Christ and his church." I can't remember a word of what the "Dominee" said, except he had a long sermon.

I was holding two Bibles that placed me squarely in the center of five generations. It was an awesome feeling and also comforting because I saw God's promise passed for many generations and spanning two oceans and several languages.

Like a documentary, our family history lay scattered around me on the floor and I was aware of God's leading for every individual represented, including Claude and I.

We were engaged for two years. With no prospect for a house, there was no chance for us to be married. Claude had gone "underground", for fear the Germans would draft him to work for the enemy , or he feared he would be transported to Germany. For a time, he repaired radios that were illegal. We were indoctrinated by Hitler's propaganda in our daily newspapers. Claude sometimes took Jews to their hiding places at isolated farms and delivered bogus or stolen food coupons or false identification papers for the underground.

When Claude heard of a hardware store asking for a manager, he applied and was accepted. His new job not only brought future security but also a home annexed to the store.

I knew he had an important message when he called me. I was working on the floor in the children's ward with sick babies in the nursery. "Amy, the German Wehrmacht will take over my house. They plan to have it occupied by a Civil Guard," he said. (These were the traitors siding with the enemy and were mostly the scum of society). "I need a marriage license. The mayor is requesting formal documentation before he will give me a housing permit."

"A marriage license?" I asked. "I am not prepared. Please, Claude, no, not yet."

"It is only a formality. We don't have to be married, but I need a permit. I will come tomorrow," Claude said.

I was in the final stage for graduation and the one requirement needed was working six weeks in the nursery.

Sister Monsma, the head nurse had an easy going manner. She was somewhat isolated from the adult world, but was level headed and usually had a twinkle in her eye, behind her thick rimmed glasses. I told her about Claude's dilemma which was now mine too. She thought this was a good story. "Amy," she said. "You may fool the Germans but not me. It will not be long and you'll be a married woman."

"No, I don't want to marry yet. I want to graduate in a few months," I said.

"Tell Claude he may come to the floor and I'll congratulate him. You two then run to the courthouse for your license," Sister Monsma said.

She told me resolutely what to do and I did not like it! "This is all because of this stupid war," I said.

The following day, Claude left with our marriage license in his pocket and I returned to the floor where Sister Monsma cornered me.

"Congratulations, Amy," she said.

"I'm not going to marry. It can wait," I said.

"You sound like me. It was years ago that I lost my chance and now I take care of sick babies. It could have been different. I might have had my own children who needed me and a loving husband."

Cuddling one of the sick babies, she left me. I thought her little babies could not have a more caring and loving nurse, and she was fun to work for too. But I wanted to graduate and travel, see what the world was like, if only for a year. Nurses were always needed on ocean liners to the Netherlands East Indies, or the Antilles.

I tried to ignore the fact that Claude was lonely. He didn't complain and he told me about making his house livable, but he didn't get on his knees asking me to marry him. I did miss him sneaking up the long stairway to my room or waiting for me at the gate.

Taking care of babies didn't have the challenge of being with adults. We were removed from the regular hospital routine. Sister Monsma kept questioning me, "Amy, how is Claude doing?"

I shrugged. It wasn't her business.

"Is your home almost finished?"

"Grandma Van Ooyen is hoping to have him settled," I said.

She was buying furniture, "for us in the future." I wasn't interested and wanted to select my own. She meant well and pots and pans were stacking up in her attic. Stores did not have much to sell, yet she was a cunning woman with many connections, and I should have been grateful. My parents made no comments, as they were occupied by sheltering a displaced Polish family who had escaped and passed the front lines for detention in Russia.

Finally Sister Monsma asked, "Amy, do you have to renew that marriage license after a certain time?"

I was not sure and said, "Claude will come, probably tomorrow because it is my birthday."

That night, realizing that I'd missed him, we talked a long time and we decided to marry on the 29th of June, only six weeks before graduation.

Sister Monsma beamed. Hugging me, she said, "I will sure miss you. We've had so much fun." She wiped her glasses sniffing, "So Claude won!"

"Yes he did, with your help; it will not be easy to tell Doctor Kruik," I said.

"He must hear it from you. Here in the hospital, we can't keep secrets very well."

I knew she would be the first one to talk. "Not now, not yet, he will be very angry with me," I said.

"You can't wait." Taking charge, she phoned his office. "Yes, Doctor Kruik, this is Sister Monsma at 'baby haven.' I've my student nurse here, Sister Hoekstra, and she needs to talk to you. No, nothing serious. She needs a little encouragement. Okay, she will be able to meet with you in about a half hour. Thank you doctor."

"Oh no! What must I say?" I groaned.

"Clean up and hurry back. We've work to do here. You gave me enough trouble." Grumbling to cover her excitement, she shoved me out the door.

Doctor Kruik must have expected quite a different problem. "Sit down Sister Hoekstra, what brings you here today?"

I hesitated, not wanting to disappoint our hospital director who we all admired for his fairness.

"Well," he said. "Do you have a problem with Sister Monsma? She can be blunt but I thought she appreciated you. The nursery is an experience required for graduation."

He did not make it any easier for me and I stammered, "I will not graduate, but will marry soon."

He hit me hard with his next question. As if he were my father, he asked, "Are you pregnant, Sister Hoekstra?"

"No doctor. I'm not pregnant."

"Then Sister, you must graduate!" he shouted angrily.

"The Germans will claim the house annex to the store he is managing," I explained.

"This is stupid, a most unreasonable excuse for marriage as I ever heard! Who is this lucky man?" he asked sarcastically.

"Sister Van Ooyen's older brother. We will marry in late June," I said.

He said, "In August you will graduate. Sister Hoekstra, we are in a terrible war. The Germans are killing our best people."

He rose, and pacing the room, turned to me again and begged, "I hope you will change your mind. We need good nurses here. You've already earned your diploma. Please stay a few months longer."

"I can't. Our plans are made. You know very well there are no homes available for young people. We are lucky," I said.

When he opened the door for me, I tried to thank him, but disregarding my hand, he said, "Your future husband could possibly be shot by the enemy."

I returned to the floor feeling cursed and a loser. Even Sister Monsma, who did her best to cheer me, could not change the fact that I had lost my goal and would never graduate with a Registered Nursing Degree.

I have saved my booklet recording my achievements, signed by the department heads. It reminds me of the wonderful happy years of training. My uniforms found a good cause, disguising Jewish people who were brought to their hiding places by the underground.

On a glorious day, June 29, 1944, the red, white and blue flag was raised on every house in our village. It told the world that Claude and I were going to get married and also gave everyone a chance to protest the German occupation, since that day was the birthday of Prince Bernhard, Queen Julianna's husband, both of whom were in exile. Flying the flag on a national holiday was strictly prohibited at the cost of retaliation, imprisonment, or death.

The old custom of raising the flag when one of the family married, gave our town a good excuse for a possible confrontation with the Civil Guards. "The daughter of Baker Hoekstra will marry today."

My father was elated by the show of colors. He took it as a personal honor and told Mother, "I will ride my bike through town and count all the flags."

She told him, "Man,"-she never called him Jacob,- "that would be rather childish."

But I knew she was very pleased with the attention, and I still see my father standing in the center of the road looking down main street saying, "Well, I can see all the flags here too," hardly containing his love for his country and me.

By 10 a.m., we rode with our parents to the Courthouse in a nearby town for the civil ceremony. Family and friends followed on bicycles, cheering and congratulating us. After a short time, we returned again to the granite stairs.

Father, pleased with the speech of a friend in the absence

Claude P. Van Ooyen
Amy J. Hoekstra

of the mayor, said, "He spoke so well. We don't have to do this over in church."

"Oh, no, this is only a promise to the state and for men," Mother said. "God has to bless them."

It would have been fine with Claude and me. We were uncomfortable in our wedding attire. My gown had been made in Paris and had been borrowed from a friend of Mother Van Ooyen who shortened the skirt with several pleats to make it fit. The satin shoes were a size eleven and stuffed with tissue paper. Claude too looked strange, in an undertaker's black tuxedo and top hat. His white shirt and gray tie belonged to the "dominee" of his mother's church. Along the shoulders of the country road, Queen's lace bloomed profusely and I wished I was wearing plain simple clothes and walking the 2 kilometers with Claude to the church ceremony.

On our return home, a pleasant surprise awaited us. All my classmates came by train from Leeuwarden to celebrate the day with me. Dressed in crisp uniforms they sang while walking several kilometers to our village. My father, noticing them first, called, "Come here Vrouw." Mother hurried, visibly touched by their solid friendship and she had tears in her eyes. "Amy, you are still one of us," my friends told me.

Class of 1944

Lunch was in the fellowship hall of the church and forming a circle around Claude and me, my friends danced, singing our silly team song:

On Sunday soup, rice and prunes
is our sister dinner for sure.
Plenty for all and a certain cure
for cleaning our bowels, we're on the go
with tissues, syringes, pills and a po.

I envied them with their black veils blowing in the wind, having exchanged mine for a white one. If some of my colleagues may have envied me, they didn't show it. Since it was a national holiday too, we all joined them in singing the national anthem, with a hastily hired photographer snapping pictures of the dancing nurses as Claude and I posed with my friends on the church lawn.

It must have taken much cooperation from the entire hospital staff for all twenty members of the graduating class to attend the wedding of one who had quit. I presumed Doctor Kruik's giving his permission was his way of showing his appreciation for me. I felt a twinge of nostalgia when my friends formed an honor guard when we entered the church, making my decision final!

The words of the minister's sermon and the old-style long-winded marriage form made no impression on me. Mother wiped her tears and I heard Father blowing his large nose, concealing his emotion. When we knelt for the blessing sung by the congregation, I thought it odd that all this ceremony was happening to us.

We had a few moments to ourselves in the privacy of a small room where we exchanged our engagement bands from the left to the right hand as is the custom. That moment is kept in my heart like Claude's name is engraved in my ring.

It was the last reunion for the class of 1944. My friends left for the six o'clock train where several worked on a night shift.

Relatives and friends in town did not need an official invitation and arrived by seven p.m. for an evening of fun, with much food and singing, and folksy poetry. Long after curfew, Claude and I biked along back country roads to our new home.

The enemy did not kill my husband, although in the first year of our marriage and the last year of World War II, we lived in constant danger of our lives.

First Year of Marriage
Last Year of War

*L*ike our grandparents and parents, Claude and I began our first day of life together by reading a chapter of the Bible after our meal. As was the custom, we would begin in Genesis and read through the whole Bible in about a year.

Claude began reading, "In the beginning God ..." Then a loud banging on the door disturbed our devotion time.

Claude opened up the store for a man dressed in black; a gold band on his arm with the letters B.W. (Burger Wacht) told him that he was a Civil Guard, a traitor siding with the enemy. Taking the gun off his shoulder, he placed it on the counter and asked for one kilo penny nails. Nails were not for sale. Those were worth their weight for bartering. There was a shortage of food, soap and everything. It was clear this man came to test the new store keeper and his loyalty to the "Regime."

Claude ignored his loud salute, "Heil Hitler!" A uniform and gun might look impressive but these men were liars without moral values. We hated them, the low characters who chose their victims at random.

Returning with a handful of used rusty nails, Claude placed them next to the man's gun. He threw some change on the counter and took the nails grumbling, "Someday you will have to pay for this."

Later in the day Claude came to me in the kitchen. His face was tightly drawn and pale. I have never seen such fear in his eyes. I asked, "What is wrong?"

"The B.W. returned with a warrant for me," he said. "Last week I placed an advertisement in the weekly paper stating we would trade that extra dining room suite that my mother bought for a rug and vacuum cleaner. The man said it was illegal and black marketing."

"That is crazy! Your Mother thought it would be a good investment even if we did not need it," I said.

"I know they'll probably confiscate it for his use. Next week I will have to appear before the judge."

We were fined nine hundred guilders in the court case, and, like Claude had said, the furniture was confiscated. So began our first week of marriage, and we were lucky that Claude was not jailed or deported to Germany!

Every day there were more restrictions, earlier curfews, and Civil Guards blocking the country roads to make life miserable for us who were hoping to buy milk and grain at nearby farms. Claude flattened a metal can to fit his body and strapped it under a heavy overcoat disguising the fact that he smuggled milk to town. Bartering was a way of life. We churned our own butter. Often friends stopped by to take their turn cranking, hoping to share in our bounty.

We had food coupons, but they were not always honored.

"Wij blikken met vast vertrouwen in de toekomst."

"We Trust in a Bright Future"

One had to stand in line for hours, returning home with whatever was available. We in Friesland were not hungry like those in other provinces, but our diet was very limited. Our coffee grinder also got a good work-out. We made our own whole wheat flour for pancakes and porridge and fried the roughly ground kernels with salt and spices in butter for a meat substitute.

104

Abonnement: Leeuwarden en Huizum
f 1.58; buiten franco f 2.26 p. 3 mnd.
Weekabonn. 13 en 18 ct. Losse nummers 5 ct. Giro 149891. Bureaux
Fr. Crt. Voorstreek 103, tel. adm. 3241,
red. 3119. Uitg. N.V. de Leeuwarder Ct.
en N.V. Leeuwarder Nieuwsblad.

Ie jaargang

FRIES

Elfjarig bestaan van de N.S.B. der Nederlanden

Plechtige herdenking te ·Amsterdam — De Rijkscommissaris en de Leider der Beweging spreken

De N.S.B. ingeschakeld in het bestuursapparaat van Nederland

DE LEIDER

Head of N.S.B
Civil Guard

Adolf Hitler

In that last winter of W.W.II, the country was divided near Arnhem where the Allied forces were defeated and the Germans tried to starve people in large cities behind the demarcation line before our liberators could proceed in the spring. They dumped food into canals and roadsides. I don't know how a ship made it into our small harbor in town, but when the word was out that bushels of beets were available at a local store, we flocked with baskets and boxes, waiting for hours in line. As luck would have it, they also had onions for sale.

We sliced, cubed and grated beets; we invented recipes, and the townspeople joked about the red delicacy with fried onions. It changed our attitude, keeping us physically and mentally fit to cope.

We also learned that ignorance was bliss. We didn't ask questions and found our own entertainment. Claude, with friends and neighbors interested in music, organized a "cultural evening."

The persons who came sneaking to our home under the cover of darkness on Thursday evenings were a motley group, and the program was as varied as the talent present. We never knew how many to expect. There were regulars who arrived early. Others came once or twice and then disappeared for awhile. They all were men who probably had fictitious names. It is possible the entertainers were English pilots who were hidden in the parsonage next door, Jews, or maybe a spying traitor. There even could have been an Angel unawares.

We used our home because, although the power was cut off by five p.m., our living room would light up very mys-

Surhuisterveen, Toren

Second House on the Left, Our Store and Home Annex

teriously while the rest of the town was in total darkness. Our musicians or those who read poetry never asked questions. I served a wholesome snack of cracked wheat dollar pancakes, sweetened with homemade beet syrup. Even if it had a very peculiar smell and a distinctive taste of sugar beets, it was the best meal all day for some of the men who came irregularly and then quietly left early.

My Aunt Anna, mother's sister who lived nearby, was the only person who could not keep her curiosity under control. On one of her visits, she asked, "Claude, tell me. Why do you have power for good lights and we must peddle our old treadle sewing machine for only a little glimmer of what I see here?"

Her husband, my Uncle John, warned, "Anna, we don't ask questions these days!"

Many did try to produce electricity by attaching a small bike light with a generator to the fly wheel of their sewing machine. As long as one kept steadily pumping, it produced a weak electrical current. Uncle John, a great story teller, enjoyed his daring tales. We did too, but some of his stories were better told in the dark. He did not want to lose his captive audience for bright lights.

Claude could not reveal his secret, so he said, " Auntie Anna, I have a large battery."

"John, why don't you think about that?" she said, implying her husband did not match up to Claude's ingenuity at all.

Uncle John, drawing on his pipe, calmly blew a huge cloud of home grown tobacco smoke. Taking a deep breath, he said, "Well, that battery is still in our car in the haystack at the farmer's place behind the sea dike. It's safe, Anna."

Aunt Anna was a persistent nagger. Usually he did not listen to her; he may have even loved her for it and often teased his wife. But she kept prodding and at last, the thought of a new adventure and a fresh daring tale made him dig up the old model T. Ford and bring the battery home.

"My Anna made me do it. It could have cost my head or I could be now in Germany and that would serve her right," he said.

Aunt Anna was delighted until not many days later the light dimmed. She kept on nagging her John and us too. Uncle John bragged of his daring trip to the farm and could tell more stories in the dark at the cost of his wife and her smart ideas that nearly cost him his life.

Claude has never told them the source of our light that truly was battery powered. A former colleague working for the telephone company had connected, at Claude's suggestion, our cable to the power generator at the substation a block from our home. It was not until our liberation in May when the German forces retreated that normal communication in the evening hours was restored to our home.

During the last winter of the war, there was no transportation available for the Germans. They raided small towns and hauled away whatever they could use. They stole our bikes which made it much harder to go out for food.

We were not frightened of the regular army. The boys were tired of war and lonely for their Heimland. But the S.S. Storm Corp, Hitler's elite soldiers, were dangerous. Their brutal retaliations caused death and destruction. Several towns were targeted, and men above the age of sixteen were mass murdered, their bodies littering intersections and highways.

Claude and I woke regularly to the sound of marching feet hitting the cobble stone pavement hard schuck, stump, schuck, stump, a loud two step rhythm and

The S. S.: Hitler's Elite Soldiers

then one day came a command, "Haltz" right in front of our house.

Claude rushed through a hole between a double wall to his secret hiding place under the floor, a dugout filled with straw, under the heavy marble store counter. I went downstairs, opening the door to an officer asking me always the same question, "Is this road leading to Mein Deutchland?"

"Nein," I told him. "A block down the road, take a right. It is approximately 50 km. to the border."

"Heil Hitler!" he saluted. But the nightly scare continued

and we wondered why this was only happening to us. Then Claude noticed a sign pointing to the bike repair shop behind our house. It looked much like the road marker at a corner. Removing the sign solved the problem, and we weren't bothered anymore until a tragedy happened.

The Germans slayed four prominent men who were working for the underground and left their bodies on a crossroad as a warning for us all. Claude repaired clandestine radios for a few who listened to the English broadcast and then printed an illegal newspaper.

When we heard a contingent of S.S. soldiers were marching in our direction, planning to round up every man and boy in town, we were prepared. Our men disappeared. The deportation of Jews in cattle trains was fresh in our minds. We hoped the heavy counter would shield Claude from piercing bayonets that probed walls and boards on the floor. In the Netherlands, there are no basements since the country is low and wet. Claude didn't have much more than two feet of breathing space as he lay on the straw on the damp soil.

The angry frustrated soldiers riddled some homes with bullets when they realized they had been fooled. I had waited for grinding feet to come to a halt. A wretched sick feeling reminded me of Eli, a Jew who had been my patient on the floor at the hospital. My stomach again protested as I was aware that escape from this madness of war was impossible. Hate became a dark wall.

Eli wore a bright yellow star of David on his pajamas as he lay in bed. When the call came for him to dress to be transported with other Jews, I dreaded telling him the news. There was no need. He knew! He looked at me proudly, and pointing to his bright yellow star, he said, "I am a Jood!" He must have read it on my face and the tears in my eyes. Trying to be brave, he said, "Sister Hoekstra, don't feel bad for me. I am an old man. Those who hate us are the ones who will perish from living with guilt."

Desperately hoping for a miracle, I tried to stall the Civil Guard. "Eli, I'll pack a lunch for you and get your medicine." It took me a long time.

On my return, he said, "Don't worry, sister. Someday you

will meet a rich man." Placing his hand on my cheek, he whispered, "I have a ten guilder gold piece and will multiply it a thousand times."

Now worried for the man's safety on the train should someone find out, I asked, "Eli, where are you hiding it?"

He pointed proudly to the star of David stitched on the left side of his shirt near his heart and said grinning, "Here Sister!"

He left knowing that he was one of God's chosen people. Not even a German dictator could change that. I and the world would never forget him.

When the S.S. soldiers stopped at the plaza in front of our store, they dispersed four by four through town. I opened the door for the officer and three of his soldiers.

He saluted sharply with a crisp "Heil Hitler." Giving orders to each of his men, he directed one to the upstairs and another to the store. He and the last one went with me to the living room and asked politely where my husband was today.

"He is gone to another town for business," I lied.

"Du canst spielen?" he asked me noticing our organ.

I shook my head nervously, fearing the worse retaliation.

"Yeah, yeah. Deutchen Meisters Das Klinging Buch, Strauss, Beethoven, Bach! Deutchland Ober allen," he laughed. "Du canst danzen?"

"Nein! Nein!" I said.

Grinning, he called on the soldier searching the store. "Du canst spielen, yeah!"

"Ah yeah!"

He ordered all three men to roll up the carpet and move the furniture to the kitchen. Politely asking for my hand, he led me on the floor. I had never danced in all my life. He must have been very good or God helped me move my unsteady feet. I danced first with him, then the other men, knowing that Claude, under the floor, would be wondering what the racket was about. I laughed and talked constantly to make him believe that he didn't have to worry about me. I hoped he would stay there crouched in his hole under the floor. I must have danced and waltzed for close to two hours in the arms from one soldier to another, pretending I was having a wonderful time while my legs wobbled in fear.

Not understanding why the soldiers were staying so long at our house, one after another, a neighbor's face peaked through the curtains in the window. Hearing the music, they left, afraid for their own safety.

Finally the soldiers assembled at the plaza. Huddled in a farm wagon drawn by two horses were two old men and a frightened group of very young boys. The captured farmer was still in shock as he held the reins of two Belgian work horses.

The officer ordered his men to straighten the rug and replace the furniture. He then thanked me and now alone with me said, "Madam, I hope your husband arrives safely home tonight."

I nodded saying, "I hope so too. I am sure he will be."

"Guttendag!" Omitting the "Heil Hitler," he rather sadly looked at the now cozy living room. I was sure that he too was tired of war.

I watched the group slowly pull out of town in a drizzly rain toward the East to Germany. A week later his prisoners walked home. They released them at the border just in time for Christmas with their families.

I had hoarded a pound of real butter and a little sugar to bake a pound cake for a welcome and the holiday season celebration. I had hidden the ingredients between the double wall near the entrance of Claude's hiding place. One of the soldiers, piercing the wall with his bayonet, found my little supply. I thanked God that the soldier's greed had misled him from looking further where he would have discovered Claude in hiding.

Worried that the S.S. Corp would return, many men left town. Claude also found shelter at the home of distant relatives until we thought it was safe to return to celebrate our first Christmas.

On our first Christmas Day together, we celebrated by drinking coffee brewed from roasted grain with a clump of chicory. We ate little whole wheat pancakes soaked in homemade sugar beet molasses and for dinner had a potato with stewed onions and a red beet salad.

Through the cold and very severe winter of 1944-45, we

lived in misery fearing imprisonment or death. Many lively bed bugs lived with us. We had no soap or disinfecting products. Luckily, I obtained several cans of scouring powder by bartering. We added this to our soft rain water, let it settle, drained it the next day, and had some suds. Often our clothes itched, and shaking the bed sheets caused dust to fly. We had a great sense of partnership that brought life-long friendships. Outwardly we were oppressed, and in bonds, inwardly free spirits defying danger.

On May 5, 1945, the German forces marched east to the border. It was a pitiful sight. We watched a once proud S.S. Corp walking behind a hay wagon carrying their weakened comrades, the defeated men of a no doubt great nation led astray by an evil dictator. They left behind a sad legacy of death and destruction for humankind all over the world.

The shadow of crosses on graves of the fallen and the ashes of Jews clouded all the festivities of liberation and happy homecomings.

Our tears developed into loud cheering when the Allied tanks rolled into town. Flags now flew with orange banners from every home. The planes overhead dropped real bread from heaven.

I danced behind the wagon carrying our musicians who during the long winter months had secretly gathered at our home.

Now they changed their repertoire to patriotic songs. Claude sat on a platform accompanying the group with all his might, pumping our little reed organ. He was the center of attention and seriously played folk tunes as if they were Bach compositions on a mighty church organ.

A few months later, on the first of August, our first child, Catherine, Alida was born in a free country that slowly rose from the dust of war.

Immigration

*I*n the years after the war, Surhuisterveen, the town where we had our hardware store, developed into a rapidly growing industrial area. During the summer of 1949, Claude was invited to a board meeting by the organizers for a new trade school. He was surprised by the presence of the director of the telephone company in Leeuwarden, who asked him, "Would you consider returning to your former position and be reinstated at the level you had when you left us? We have a need for dependable employees with experience."

He offered Claude a full compensation for the years he had resisted the enemy and for the loyalty to his country. It was tempting. We now had three daughters, Kathy, our Anne born in 1946, Janice in 1948; and I was again pregnant. Trusting God for our plans, we decided to put the business up for sale.

I was happy to move to Leeuwarden. Many of my former friends, now graduated, found work in the area. Actually, I resented all business activities. Living in the annex to the store, it reminded me of the irregular hours living at home.

Late in January, we moved to a new house on the Karel Doorman Street, and two days later, our first son Peter was born. Claude proudly said, "Well son, you will have a good spanking should you misbehave."

"A fine welcome," I said, not believing we had a boy. I told the nurse, "Show me, I want to see him before you put a diaper on him."

Claude's sister and her husband had immigrated to the United States. For sometime, she was a visitor in the U. S. and during the Korean War, their temporary visitor's permit was canceled. Returning to the Netherlands, they reapplied for permanent citizenship. She also included all her family, although I had no intention of leaving my cozy home.

We had a steady income and a nice house located behind a small park. The older children were in kindergarten, and I had made new friends. For me life was perfect that first year. I ignored my husband's unhappiness. Claude was quiet and in his spare time played the organ. He and Mr. Johann S. Bach were inseparable. Although Bach lived three hundred years before him, they were close friends and had a definite understanding. Claude played his compositions on the organ when he came home from work, during his long dinner break at noon and until late at night.

And Mrs. Bach and I also had many things in common. She had at one time married her second cousin and so did I. Could it be that Mr. Bach, the master composer and organist woke his wife with music early in the morning when she wanted to sleep?

How often I have awakened to Bach's music played by Claude on our small reed organ in the front room of our home in the Netherlands!

Mrs. Bach had many children and so did I. Claude serenaded a new baby with organ music in its tiny ears as soon as they were born. He turned to his friend, Mr. Johann S. Bach, and together they rejoiced, giving thanks to God for the blessing of a new life.

I did not realize how unhappy Claude was until his cousin and friend of his youth, living in Gorredyk, visited the United States. He returned with much enthusiasm, telling us of the immigrant's opportunities.

I was shocked when one evening Claude came home from work and said, "Today on the bulletin board, I read a notice that South Africa has a need for instrument makers. They have the same telephone system that we use here in our country."

"Oh, what will that mean for us?" I asked.

"I've been thinking to apply at the African embassy for the position," he said.

"Why, when you do the exact same work now. It doesn't make sense to me."

"Because I've been away from this job. Those who were on my level are now department heads. It's not easy for me." He explained that in a new situation he may have better opportunities.

"I don't want to immigrate to an entirely different country. We would have to find new roots again, and what will be the future of our children?" I asked.

"It would not be difficult to communicate. You make friends easily and both Dutch and the English language is spoken," Claude said.

Immigration was the topic of the day. Nobody wanted to face the prospect of going through another war. Korea, a country we hardly knew, was fighting and lives were lost in Indonesia, our former Dutch territory. Thousands were leaving for the United States or Canada. I did everything possible to keep Claude more happy. I knew he was not and probably would never be, but I was determined to fight for my home and cozy existence in familiar surroundings.

In our correspondence with my sister-in-law, I casually mentioned that Claude had thoughts of applying to the telephone company in South Africa.

When a letter arrived from her, she wrote it would be irresponsible for us to leave Claude's mother and his brother in the Netherlands. She wrote, "It is much more sensible for you to come to the U.S. In the future, that would make it possible for the two to visit us here."

She suggested we ask at the American Consulate for our registration number so that a possible immigration might be honored soon. Claude's sister is one who is ahead of what may happen. She is not one to leave anything to chance.

"We don't speak a word of English! How will we ever communicate over there?" I asked Claude.

A man who had recently returned from the U.S. was very disappointed with the American lifestyle. He told me, "It is a land where you have to take care of yourself, unless you speak their language, which is English. There are opportunities for work, but they don't pay in cash. They give a 'paycheck' and you have to go to a bank to exchange it for money. Then there are bills, bills and more bills."

I had asked him, "What are bills?"

"It is the only word I learned, light bills, gas bills, water bills, telephone bills. I think for some it may be a good life if there were not all those bills."

How would I ever manage those bills without speaking English? Our meter man collected directly in cash and the baker, a delivery man from the grocery store, and the milkman stopped by daily at our house.

When the man told me that most purchases were made with credit and that at the stores one would say "Charge it," I thought life in the United States was too complicated for me.

Claude was not persuaded. He decided to call the Embassy for the state for our registration. "At least that is free," he said.

We quickly received a reply with forms attached. We were first in line for immigration.

Stunned, but not easily giving in, I told Claude, " Not everyone is a good candidate for immigration. Why don't you ask for a psychological test by the counselor of your company?"

He agreed and made an appointment. I was sure that the doctor would tell him it was a very foolish idea to leave for an uncertain future in a strange country.

I was wrong! The doctor said he wished to speak with me too. "This is an undertaking you both must agree to," he told Claude.

Reluctant, I made an appointment for myself, hoping to reason with the man and making it clear to him that life was good in the Netherlands. We were lucky to own a home and had everything one needs to be happy. Mentally well prepared for what to say, I found myself in the counselor's office. He began by saying, "You have married an intelligent man. His test shows he has many talents."

I nodded and waited suspiciously for what he was going to say next, ready to prove my point. He then hit me hard by stating, "You would not like to see your husband's talents wasted on preplanned blueprints and boring details, I hope."

"What do you mean by that?" I asked

"The job he has now gives him no opportunity or room for creativity. He works for the government. They insist he follow rules and regulations."

"Oh? Maybe, but if you advise us to immigrate to a foreign country where neither of us can speak the language, that surely will be a big problem!" I said.

"You don't need to take that chance, but I can guarantee you by age fifty your husband will probably be a grouchy, unmotivated dull man and you will have to live with him."

Ouch! Tears sprung in my eyes because the doctor did not give me a chance to tell him of my feelings. I looked for my hanky. "Here, take mine." He took a clean hanky from his drawer. "I haven't been easy on you," he began. "Your husband told me about your solid marriage relationship. You are a lucky woman. Maybe someday you will thank me."

He did not convince me. I felt trapped and left without any appreciation for the counselor's advice.

We filed our application with the Embassy in the Hague, I was hoping for a delay or a miracle. Claude's sister found a sponsor for the next five years for us who was to guarantee a sum of

The Van Ooyen Family one Month before Immigrating
3-17-51
Amy (29), Claude (36), Peter (15 mo), Ann(4), Janie (3), Kathy (5)

five thousand dollars so we would not be dependent or a burden to the government in our new country until we could apply for naturalization.

Mr. Ronda, our sponsor, set aside a one hundred thousand dollars security fund, and our applications were processed with priority within a month.

The night before we were to leave for our physicals in Amsterdam, Kathy had a fever. I isolated her from the other three children. When she undressed in the office of the American physician, her body had sprouted a genuine case of chicken pox. I did not understand the doctor and told him she only had "Water pox." He did not know what they were and I had my first bout of misunderstanding a person, feeling stupid and apprehensive of all Americans when he showed a definite disgust for us. It postponed our departure for a month, and once home, I tried to forget that our house was for sale and also most of what was precious to me.

The day did come when people rushed to our house. They came even before the advertising was listed in the paper, having heard we were planning to leave soon. We were run over by bargain hunters who, like pirates, grabbed our belongings, plundering our home. The kitchen curtains were taken down and with a heavy doormat, a woman threw a wad of bills into the pot I held. My brooms went with the mirror in the hall, our children's beat up toys were sold too high. I was in a daze collecting the money. A wrought iron coat hanger with beautiful Delft ceramic tiles, a wedding gift from Claude's relatives, was almost too heavy for one woman to carry. "I always wanted one like it," she shouted. I did not even count what she paid for it.

My neighbor and a very good friend asked, "Amy, may I have your beautiful Anturium plant? I'll take good care of it, trust me."

Knowing she'd treasure my plant, I told her, "Claude gave me the plant as a housewarming gift when we came to live here. I give it to you for the wonderful time we've had together."

My eyes were dry until a woman made a bid for our beautiful solid oak dining room furniture with hand carved buffet doors. It brought a very good price, but the memories of so many meals served, giving thanks for the bartered food during the war made it hard to part with.

Two men passed me, dragging our heavy wooden wringer washer through the kitchen door. I sat down, exhausted on a wooden crate and wept, not knowing if it was for myself or Claude when he played a few bars on his little organ that would have to be put into storage. There was not enough room for the instrument on the ocean liner or for his friend, Mr. Johann S. Bach.

Tears dropped on the money, lots of money heaped in a bowl on my lap. Claude saw me cry and he said, "We must give thanks, Amy. Everything is sold."

"Thanks? Thanks for what? My home is empty and so am I!"

"We had a terrific sale. In the last three hours we made enough money to pay half for our passage and now there is enough left for the amount of dollars we are allowed to take with us too. In a few weeks we sail to America," he said.

I knew he was right. So many people were forced to give away their possessions. Sitting on a crate, Claude gave thanks, but I pretended to do so! In the crate were a minimum of household goods, our bedding, linens, dishes and the heirlooms that Tante Aaltje and Mother had given me. There was the tea service, the wedding gift to my grandmother from Claude's grandfather, who were twins, also a pewter coffee server from my flamboyant grandfather Roel VanderWal, which was given to him after directing the town choir for twenty five years.

The crate held the baptismal dress of our four children and family pictures. For me, it did not make sense to give thanks to God. Only a few hours before, we had a home and now I held a bowl with money that must be the payment for leaving all that was dear to me and everyone I loved. I understood that Claude looked toward the future, but for me, life was uncertain. I wished to be with my children who were cared for by our parents. We were free for a last visit to our friends and relatives during the weeks before our departure.

When we regrouped as a family again, we said goodbye to Pake Hoekstra, nearly ninety years old. He was prepared to give us a fine farewell. We all knew that between the two bed closets in his living room was a china closet and on the top shelf a flask with Beppe's raspberry brandy. This very special treat had been saved since her death. On this day Pake presented us with a solemn toast. He wished us God's blessing on the long journey to a strange country and a different continent.

A tear trickled along his large Hoekstra nose when he strained the "Salie Molke" (sage milk), adding lots of sugar for the children. "You must drink it hot," he said, his voice quivering.

I knew his thoughts. "It is a good medicine against cold and it will take care of possible worms, a good preventative on the long trip."

"Pake, will you play your organ for us?" Claude said, hoping Pake would find comfort in his music.

His hands were shaking. Paging through one of his music books, he chose Melodies for the Harmonium, compositions by Herman Wenzel. Stopping at a notation "Mooi" (beautiful) in his own handwriting, he placed his old arthritic hands on the keys. The tender voice of the old reed organ translated Pake's feelings when he poured all his love for us into the music.

"I played this piece for Beppe many times," he said. "Now, Claude, it is your turn."

Claude shook his head, "No, Pake." The memory of this fine moment was too precious for a possible discord.

Today, almost fifty years later, Claude is using Pake's music books, playing the same pages for preludes at church services here in Ironwood. He especially favors the pieces marked by Pake's beautiful handwriting, "Mooi!" Claude inherited the books on one of our visits to the Netherlands.

I watched my mother pack the children's suitcases on the day before our departure. She folded the small garments of our children with a last loving touch.

Observing her, I promised my Mem I would write her weekly and tell her in detail about our children. She chose to say her good byes cheerfully at the home of Claude's mother, where, no doubt, the two women tried to comfort each other that day.

On the morning of April 17, 1951, my father, sister, and

younger brother brought us to the train. Father ran along the moving train to the very end of the platform, waving with a white hanky, his arms milling frantically in the chilly air. He displayed an ultimate helplessness of losing the race. I hurt for him in desperation.

Arriving at Rotterdam, the *S.S. New Amsterdam* , flagship of the Holland America line, towered with its two smoke stacks above the many seafaring vessels at Europe's busiest harbor. We hugged our relatives, my sister Janke and brother Piet, and Ralph, the baby of our family. I wished to shout, "Not yet! No, I am not leaving!" But a steward came when I hugged my Uncle Onne.

"Hurry, passengers are to check in for boarding," the man shouted above the noise.

I told the steward who carried our two older children on board, "I am amazed at the size of this ship."

"Ma'am, on the ocean, she is not large," he said. Sensing some of his apprehension, I worried.

We lined up at the railing, trying to find the faces of our relatives in the crowd. When one loud blast gave the first warning that we were ready to leave, Janie covered her ears and started to cry. I took her into my arms and watched the people wave their farewell. There was a second blast; Kathy and Anne, scared now, also cried. Claude held the screaming Peter who was frightened by the commotion.

Black smoke billowed from the two stacks. The dark mass of people now faded; it seemed as if the shore was moving and we settled in our cabin. Our homeland disappeared.

Our experienced steward told me, "I will watch your children. Dinner is now served on the main deck."

I had overheard him saying, "They have their hands full with four small children, but the mother handles it well." He gave me encouragement which I desperately needed for the days ahead.

Arriving at our table, the smell of the food made me sick. I knew immediately that I would not be a very good sailor and returned to the cabin where the steward asked, "What can I do for you, Ma'am?"

Feeling miserable, I said, "Leave me alone to die."

"You're not really sick, only a little seasick," Claude told me, not giving me much sympathy. For the first time in his life he had tasted turkey with all the trimmings and was still smacking his lips.

"The sea is a little rough. Would a cup of tea or a soft drink make you feel better Ma'am?" our concerned steward asked.

I tried his advice but the huge waves rolled and swayed our ship and I lay nauseated and dizzy in my bunk. The children went to the nursery and Claude sat on deck, enjoying the scene of massive waves attacking the ship. With its powerful engines, it plowed steadily across the Atlantic ocean depths, setting course for our new country.

Before the children went to bed in the evening, the steward came again asking, "What must I serve the children, Ma'am?"

"Oatmeal, give them a bowl of oatmeal," I 'd say.

Today our older children have one memory of crossing the Atlantic ocean. "We had to eat oatmeal, a bowl of thick oatmeal every night!"

Several people dining with Claude suggested that I go on deck and take a breath of fresh air. One was a pastor who traveled with his family to a new assignment at a church in New Jersey. He conducted our evening devotions, and on one of his pastoral visits, he said, " You must try to eat."

I turned green and retched in his presence. Quickly leaving, he promised, "I will pray for you this evening."

I had not dared to go on deck for fear of jumping ship but at Claude's urging, I went. He brought the children from the nursery. Janie, who had darted ahead, escaped our eye and the three year old climbed a wire fence to the top of the ship's railing. I wanted to scream. Mustering all my self control, I watched Claude carefully lift our girl from the danger of falling overboard.

Delayed a day by the storm at sea, we entered the harbor of Hoboken, and everyone went to the upper deck, greeting the Statue of Liberty. Cheering loudly, the excited passengers waved at the "Great Lady," and I puked at her. Too miserably sick for an apology, I watched the ship tugged to shore.

Claude carried our Peter and the large manila envelope containing our papers, health certificates, and X.R's. I made sure the girls were not lost, strapping the three in leather halters. Having sympathy for our tight little group, the security officer stamped our passports, and we quickly passed through customs without the usual questioning.

Weakened and unstable on my feet, I looked for our six suitcases in a large hall. There, with a group of men, one young man spotted me, "Is that you, Ymkje?" he said. Surprised to hear my name, I recognized him, Hank VanderHeide, a classmate who had attended our school in Lutjegast.

"Hank, you have changed," I said.

He was smartly dressed in casual sports clothing. I then remembered that he had emigrated to New York several years before us.

"You have changed too, I can't believe you have four beautiful children," he said.

He took Janie and one of our suitcases. The other man took Kathy and Anne and the rest of our luggage. I heard Hank converse in English with his friends and change quickly to Dutch as he spoke with us.

When I told him that I was worried about learning a new language, he laughed. "You will find many who speak Dutch in Grand Rapids, Michigan. It's almost like the 'old country.'" I thought he sounded odd, not realizing he was an American citizen now.

"We'll have lunch in the Christian Seaman's Home, and later I'll take you to Grand Central Station to make sure you are on the right train," he promised.

My appetite returned. Thankful for a safe arrival and Hank's assistance, I bowed my head for prayer, not understanding a word of what the director of the establishment said. I peeked and watched the ship's pastor, Reverend Van Oostdorp and his family struggling with their heavy suitcases. He took a deep breath before opening the door.

Nudging Hank, I said, "Hank, that is the pastor who led our

services on board."

I had an inkling something was wrong when I heard Hank say, "The other man will take care of the reverend. The men must have thought Claude was the new pastor who we were to welcome. I was so surprised to see you Amy, I forgot to introduce Claude."

The real pastor also was heartily welcomed by the church delegation and we bowed our head again to thank God for the families' safe arrival and ask a second blessing for the food. Claude sat across the table from me and he smiled. Looking very handsome in his navy blue suit, I thought he could easily have passed for a "reverend."

In contrast to what I was told, we had a great welcome to America. The lady who ran the restaurant packed us a free lunch on the long train ride to Michigan and wished us success.

Once on the train, I worried that we might pass our destination. Again, a very friendly conductor tried to explain to us, "We will not arrive in Grand Rapids until 11 A.M. in the morning. You may rest for a few hours."

I watched the landscape; sometimes with open spaces, sometimes hilly and sometimes large rivers winding their way. It was so different from the straight canals and lowlands I was used to. The land looked as if it were uninhabited, compared to my crowded country where every inch of soil is used and made productive.

Claude's sister and our sponsors, Mr. and Mrs. Arthur Ronda, welcomed us at the Grand Rapids depot. I could not understand what Mrs. Ronda said, but thought she asked me, "Is your name Amy?"

Wanting to please her, I said, "Yes," and received my new American name.

Mr. Ronda, not knowing very much Dutch, tried to be friendly to Claude, slapping him on the shoulder, he greeted him, "Hey, you old 'Smeerlap'!" It is a bad slang word in Holland and is translated, "you dirty liar!"

I thought it quite a difference from being mistaken for a pious minister of the gospel at our arrival in Hoboken.

Our generous sponsor decided to buy us a house on land contract; and a few days later, we moved to 525 Hall street S.W. in Grand Rapids where our neighbors said we were "the new green Dutchies" living on the corner.

Main Deck of S.S. New Amsterdam

525 Hall Street S.W.

*W*e were aware that we had lost our roots and an ocean lay between all that was familiar. The former owner of the house had suddenly died and his wife was ailing. The children sold their home furnished; chairs and tables were arranged as if waiting for their return.

The drawn shades, draped by dark silk curtains were closed. When we entered the stuffy interior of our future home, I thought I was in a museum. Old-fashioned overstuffed brown horsehair furniture with sagging springs had been dressed up with many hand crocheted doilies. A silk lamp shade on a beautiful antique oriental base was standing near an empty bird cage, robbed of life and song.

We found death on the pillows in the bedroom, bloodstains explaining the man must have died from a stroke. His pipe lay on a fine marble ashtray, the tarry smell adding to the gloomy atmosphere. I was appalled and decided we would never find one good restful night of sleep there.

Claude pried open the stuck window, hoping to whisk the morbid stink from the room; but when the pungent fragrance of an old blooming spirea bush, drifted into the room, complimenting the somber discovery, I said, "Pew! I will never again like the smell of those flowers!"

"Why?" Claude asked when he returned from the basement taking inventory of what was stored there. "We will cut down those bushes and soon," I thought, and decided to inspect the kitchen. Here I found unfamiliar utensils that I didn't know how to use: the recipes in a box were for cups; tablespoons, and teaspoons; and all the spices had strange names; I had to smell what they were. In Holland, we used scales and measured in grams. I did like the roomy light kitchen. It was a cheery place, and a square oak table with an enamel top and matching chairs

525 Hall Street S.W.
Grand Rapids, Michigan

were very practical.

Claude returned in a silly mood, wearing the dead man's thread worn sweater . He had knotted a clean red workman's hanky on four corners on his head. "Didn't find good tools. The man was not a tinkerer," he said.

"Please take off that sweater." It was a reminder of the contaminated bedroom.

I tore it from his shoulders but he laughed, "There is a lot of warmth in it yet. It's cold down there. Those people were pack rats!"

I thought he should help me clean the kitchen and wash the ceiling, but he went down again to a man's domain, hoping to discover more tools and odds and ends, only he could use.

I brewed coffee, washed a few dishes and thought about calling him but changed my mind, wondering why he was staying down there that long. Going downstairs, I found him in the furnace room looking at an old magazine. "Come and see," he said.

It was a Dutch weekly from September, 1918 called <u>De Spiegel</u> (The Mirror) . On the center page was a photograph of a

The Train Wreck at Wezep September 13, 1918
Picture Found on May 17, 1951 in our First Home in the USA
The Van Ooyen Tragedy

train wreck, the worst in Netherlands history in which Claude's father Pieter Klaas Van Ooyen and his brother Wiebe both were killed on the 13th of September, 1918. The train was lying on its side on the twisted rails and two of the coaches were partially buried in mud near the Merwede canal. The dike carrying the railway gave way after torrential rains near a bridge spanning the waterway at the town of Wezep. Claude kept staring at the picture. "Amy, under one of those white sheets covering the lined up biers lies my father," he said, in disbelief as he searched for the body of his father.

Pieter (left) and Wiebe

"My mother was pregnant with my younger brother who was born a week after the accident, on the twentieth of September. The relatives must have hidden this picture from us because I have never seen it. My brother was named after the two men, Pieter Wiebe," Claude said.

Only God knew the reason why the Van Ooyen family tragedy followed us to the one home in Grand Rapids, Michigan where someone saved an old news article on this large continent as a remembrance of this national disaster. Did one of their relatives also die there?

The people were former Dutch immigrants. A large box in a dark corner of the basement bore the name of the family. I read, Jelles, July 1905; and they had come with the Holland America Line, the S.S. New Amsterdam, as we had. Our crate with the same markings was waiting for inspection by the custom officers from Muskegon before we could open it. It had our name and arrival date also, 1951!

In the evening when Claude was working at a factory nearby, I cleared out the stuffy drawers in a massive buffet where I found their family records. Here Jelles stored financial statements and personal letters. Dealings with a bank in Amsterdam were in the Dutch language, explaining the transfer of funds forwarded from Johannesburg, South Africa. Snooping further through the papers of a man who died gave me a guilty feeling. Mr. Jelles wrote a lovely poem for his wife after the death of their young son. It was the cry of a grieving father trying to comfort his wife after leaving their first-born in a small grave under the burning hot sun in a strange country. A picture of that grave was pinned to the yellow paper. They must have returned to the Netherlands when the "Boer War" raged with the British in South Africa .

"Now, almost a half century later, life is repeating itself," I said to Claude, as he looked through the old correspondence the people had saved.

"At least we've been spared the South African experience," Claude said. "I told you they were pack rats."

I wondered if it could happen that a total stranger might someday snoop through our records and letters that we saved of those dear to us in Holland and then throw them out as junk and burn our precious memories. I gathered what seemed special and gave that it the woman who rented the upstairs apartment from us. She would know what to do with it or pass it on to the family. Maybe it had been overlooked by them.

Hoping that our children would someday have a better sense of values, I stored our documents in a strong box even though Claude did not think they were important. "We will make a fresh start here in the States," he said.

While in a thorough cleaning mood, many valuable antiques went in the garbage. The very cumbersome and heavy furniture looked odd and outdated to me. A fine French secretoire, the oak dining room set, the old ice box, and a beautiful ornate bedroom suite disappeared from the side porch. There were also stacks of books and three worn English Bibles. The grubby garbage man knocked on the back door and said, "Lady, this is not junk. I refuse to dump God's Word!" Speaking English mixed with Dutch, I suppose that he was very disappointed with me.

Nodding to make him understand that I had probably made a mistake, I tried to explain to him that they did not mean much to me. I could not read them, but his gestures and angry scolding were telling me clearly that I was going to hell and would be damned. Handing the Bibles to me, he said, "God help you!" It was my first English lesson and I'll never forget it!

Our house on the corner of Caulfield Ave. and Hall Street did not have much of a yard for the children to play in. We had a neighbor behind us, a widow, Mrs. Oosterban. Next to us lived an elderly lady, Mrs. Emaus. Four children moving into their quiet existence entertained them.

At first, they liked to hear our three-year-old Janie speak Dutch, bribing her with cookies and candy. She could not understand what they told her but blabbered on happily collecting her bounty. She was frustrated too. She asked me, "Mom, do you know people here cannot talk?"

Later, she was the first to speak English and forgot Dutch. The neighbors stopped rewarding her, and in her own way, she got even. "Here, take them," she said, giving me a handful of tulips.

"Where did you get those pretty flowers?' I asked.

She happily said, "I took them. They aren't nice to me anymore. I talk to them but they don't give me cookies. I picked them for you, Mommy."

Finally, customs opened our crate and the few pieces of furniture, plain and small, were lost in our large room between the overstuffed couch and chairs. The children, happy to see some of their toys, played with them before I tucked them in bed. Claude worked the night shift and I, alone now, began to feel sorry for myself, a displaced person. Sadly lying alone in my bed, waiting for Claude to come home, I watched the moon rising above the very old maple trees on Hall Street. I thought of the same moon shining on my cozy little home in the Karel Doorman Street. I took some courage and made a bargain with God telling Him that I would stay in the United States for five years. If by then, I did not feel this was my home, I would return. Knowing I had given God and Claude five years, I slept well.

For days I told the two nosy widows behind the back yard fence, "When the house is clean, I will invite you over for coffee." The morning they came, our sunny kitchen was bright and the coffee smelled good. It was a fine house warming party with the cookies and orange raisin cake they made. (I still have the recipes.) The ladies must have been disappointed that I removed the doilies and they asked where they were. I gladly gave those to them to sort out and put on their chairs. "Yes," they agreed. "Young people live next door now."

"Did you find any money?" Mrs. Emaus asked.

We had, but I didn't tell her it was all of forty-six cents.

The following week, she brought me a pumpkin pie. I thought it looked very unappetizing. "This is called a pie," she said. " In Dutch it is spelled and could be pronounced like "pee"! Don't ever say that, Amy. Don't make that mistake.. A new immigrant woman went to the bakery and asked for one of those Apple pees! They still joke about it!"

I was lucky both women spoke Dutch with a definite dialect from the province of their parents. Mrs. Oosterban was from Zeeland and Mrs. Emaus from the province of Gronigen. I had much good advice and practical English lessons from these ladies. They also gladly babysat for us. When I told them that we had "smashed potatoes" and that on Sundays we ate dinner "on" the dining room table, the lesson was demonstrated. Mrs. Emaus sat on the table. "On the table, like this?" she asked. I was a quick learner. We dumped her pumpkin pie. Claude thought it was not worth the cream she made it with.

Since we did not own a car, we attended an English-speaking church nearby. People were friendly but avoided conversation. A few older folks invited us over, but the younger people were shy.

Our young pastor's wife took courage and asked if she could come for an afternoon's visit to acquaint herself with our family. She did not speak a word of Dutch and that made us both nervous. Silently, we drank our first little cup of tea, smiling timidly at each other and both searching for a topic of common interest. Having learned a few English words, I thought about my neighbors who gave me their favorite recipes. In broken English, I asked, "A cake recipe?"

She brightened and smiling happily answered, "Oh yes! What cake recipe do you like best? I have a very good Devil's Food cake recipe and also one for an Angel Food cake I gladly share."

Embarrassed by her descriptive language, I thought about my strict Mother. She would wash my mouth with soap and I would get a tongue lashing too when I mentioned Satan's name. Here this sweet pastor's wife flippantly spoke of the devil, naming the angels with a cake all in one breath. Deciding an angel cake sounded better for right now, I asked for that recipe.

"It takes eleven egg whites," she began. That again startled me, almost a dozen eggs. What would I do with the yokes? We each only had one egg for breakfast on Sunday. Politely writing down the ingredients, I knew this cake was not for us and wished I'd asked for the devil's food cake, thinking it would be sinful to use eleven eggs in a cake. Now I began to understand why many immigrants went to a church that scheduled Dutch services.

We were hoping to learn the English language, so we did not change to another church. People were friendly. I had met a lady in church who asked me several times, "Come over sometime Amy." It happened again and again and I finally asked her, "When do you expect me to come?"

"Oh, sometime," she said casually.

It then dawned on me that it was only an American expression of friendliness. It made me disappointingly lonely for a day, and I found comfort from my elderly neighbor friends.

Claude, working in a factory for small wages, was paid forty dollars a week. On Saturdays he did yard work for a dollar an hour in East Grand Rapids, riding an old bike for hours with a spade tied to its frame. I often thought of him leaving neatly dressed to go to his office at the telephone company in Leewwarden. We now could not even afford to buy a pair of jeans. At first he wore a dress suit in the factory until he was nicknamed, the "Dominee", the Pastor, so we scrounged enough money for cotton pants.

We were thrifty and with the rent of "Aunt Jessie" who lived in the apartment upstairs, the house payments were low. We had adjusted to the large corner house and kept the yard tidy. Claude transplanted the spirea bush to Mrs. Emaus' backyard. She said she loved smelling the flowers. Both the front and back porch had new flower boxes with red geraniums and white petunias. I had planted blue morning glories that climbed the railings of a trellis. Mowing the lawn on a beautiful summer day, struggling to keep the heavy click-clacking machine on the decline of the bank, I noticed a young woman who had passed our home several times. I waved and she smiled sadly, looking as if she was expecting me to talk to her. I asked, "How are you?"

She said, "Are you Dutch? They've told me you are not homesick and I should talk to you. I've been past here many

1953

134

times, but you are always so busy. My name is Jennie."

"No, I keep busy. Come in for a cup of tea. I will quit for awhile," I said.

She began to weep, tears flowing freely, telling me of immigrating with her parents to North Dakota where they worked on a farm for very small wages and plenty of food shared by their boss. She had married and her husband now had a good paying job. "I miss my family and am so alone," Jennie sobbed.

"Do you have hobbies to keep busy?" I asked, hoping she would stop crying. I tried to imagine how it might be if I were in her situation, but she snapped, "Don't give me advice. People constantly tell me what I must do. We want a baby and I don't get pregnant!" Jennie was very ignorant and naive, telling me of intimate old wives' tales that had been suggested to her, trying to explain what prevented her from getting pregnant.

She said, "I thought since you have four young children, you may know." Looking expectantly at me as if I had the secrets for fertility, she spilled tears as fast as words.

"You are too tense, too eager. Relax. I've read it can be a possible cause for infertility when one is tense and stressed," I kindly managed to say.

"What must I do? Please tell me! We've done everything and nothing happens," she sobbed. I thought Jennie did have a problem. It seemed hopeless but I repeated, saying, "I feel you should try to do something different. I mean a new hobby, plant a garden, sing in a Dutch choir, go visit the elderly in the Holland home and learn to speak and write English."

It was too much for Jennie. She stopped crying, and I thought I had given her a few ideas, but she asked, "May I come and visit you again?" I think she hoped pregnancy was contagious!

"Anytime you need encouragement. But then you must tell me that you have found a new interest or a hobby. I almost guarantee that next year you'll have a new baby. " It sounded hopeful, but when Jennie left me, she was doubtful and sad. It seemed my advice for her was lost.

Not really, she did not get pregnant but my advice helped me! When I told the children that we were expecting a baby,

Anne, concerned that her father was not informed about the family happenings, asked, "Mommy, does Daddy know?"

I assured her that first I had told Dad. "Now you all must keep the surprise a secret from your friends for awhile."

Our quiet Kathy forgot her promise, when a school friend dashed into our kitchen one morning. Her friend was all excited, telling the girls of her great news. Dancing in circles around the kids eating their breakfast, she said, "Hear this, what we bought last night. We've a new car, a brand new 1954 Buick. It's dark red and my Dad won't let Mom drive it!"

Our children tried to absorb the news since we had also bought our first "new car," a 1941 Chrysler with a big dent on the right rear fender and rusty worn running boards. We parked it close to the curb so the neighbors would not see the big dent, and I polished the black paint to a rich shine.

Our First Car in the U.S.A 1941 Chrysler
(with dent hidden by tree)

Kathy spoke first, spilling her great news and saving the family reputation, "Well, Carol, we've a surprise too. We are going to have a brand new baby and it will be a 1954 Model!"

Three years of my "five year plan" with God had passed

when, in May, our new "American 1954 Model" arrived a day after Mother's Day on May 10th, three days before my birthday. I decided to back quietly out of our covenant and enjoy life in the United States. Claude didn't know about my five-year trial time. He had been too busy working. He found a tool and die shop where the owner, a German, understood the educational value of his college diploma in the Hague. He now earned better wages, and we were able to make double payments on the land contract for our home.

Our Judith May was well worth the bill we paid for her birth. The doctor charged us seventy-five dollars, a week's wages. The insurance refunded us eighty dollars, so our Judy was a five dollar bonus!

The day I brought her home our house was filled with purple lilacs. Claude had literally plundered the blooming bush behind our home and the fragrance still reminds me of her. She has told me purple is her favorite color and I understand the reason behind it-she was a little princess.

Now with five children, our home became a little too crowded. We also needed a large yard where the children had room to play. It was time to sell our house on Hall Street.

We paid everything we bought with cash, shying away from credit cards. The idea of saying "charge it" made me feel dependent.

The housing market had dropped and we would lose money on our house. The impatient realtor agent suggested that Mr. Ronda, our sponsor, may have sold us the house for a profit. We needed a good down payment for another home because we had not acquired a credit rating. My conservative reasoning dealt us a blow.

"Nobody is so generous, buying a home for a family, like you claim. This man must be a fool. I'll be here at seven-thirty this evening and you give me your answer by asking your sponsor to drop a thousand dollars off the contract for the down payment you need," he said.

Claude told me, "We'll pray about this." But he made it clear that we would trust the honesty of our benefactor and sponsor, Arthur Ronda.

By seven-thirty, a person knocked on the kitchen door. The realtor agent was at the front door, and when the two men met in the dining room, they knew each other. I listened to their conversation in disbelief. The sale was made within a half hour. We did not have to show the house, and we got the price we had asked.

We have experienced many answers to our prayers but this was a true miracle.

We lived in tents for the summer of 1955 at Olin Lake, waiting for the F.H.A. loan to be processed due to the tight money situation and our lack of financial experience. That year I also applied for a credit card and learned to say, "Charge it!"

Claude worked many overtime hours. We started a savings account at a bank where I paid the bills now and balanced my checkbook.

We had a glorious summer camping. One night it "rained" little frogs, dozens of frogs plastered our tent where they must have caught small bugs falling from the trees by moonlight. We swam and fished, explored the woods, had campfires, caught cicadas and ate dozens of watermelons cooled in an ice cold spring.

Finally, we received our approval for a loan of $11,900 on a 4 1/4 % interest rate for twenty years. On the Saturday of Labor Day weekend, we moved to 3710 Cheyenne Drive in Grandville. I missed the wind whispering in the trees, the little creatures of the night scurrying around the tent, and even wondered if the large blue racer snake was sleeping peacefully in the sand below the hill on Olin Lake.

We now had a large yard with weeds and wild flowers growing between the remnants of an old railroad track. Our kids had found a path that led to a gravel pit. They called it the Indian Trail. For them, it is still "our" home. For us, now living in the U.P. of Michigan, it is the house Down-State.

Our First Summer at 3710 Cheyenne Dr.

I followed my mother as she inspected the interior of our new home. Glancing at the old-fashioned brown couch, she straightened the throw hiding bare spots and with a hint of disappointment, said, "I see, here in America too, you must do with what you have."

The old furniture we inherited with the house on Hall Street looked shabby. Had I been too optimistic in my weekly letters written to our parents? Were they misled? We had saved and paid for my parent's trip to the United States. Our reasoning was that after a five-year absence, they must be eager to see their grandchildren. Other immigrants, friends and relatives, took their family for a vacation to the Netherlands where envious relatives welcomed them as successful immigrants.

Our parents, now retired, made the trip on a ship because my father did not want to fly. We drove our late model Studebaker sedan to New York, and now, after five years, we were waiting at the dock in Hoboken for their arrival. The memories were still fresh, but we had changed. I had a new awareness of the obvious expression of anxiety on some of the immigrant's faces.

Late in the evening we had come home. Friends had cared for the children and our home looked bare without them. I heard my mother say, "Well, one can't expect to be rich in only a few years."

Driving through Canada from the East, my parents had asked us to stop at friends from their hometown. The bleak wide-open spaces had intimidated them, and when we arrived at the dilapidated farm house miles from town, mother had said, "I hope you live in a nicer area, Amy." She was clearly worried. I had assured her we lived on a paved street in a new section of town, but hadn't told her that the upstairs rooms were not finished yet and that the children slept under the rafters.

The family in Canada had great ideals and plenty of room in that large house that they were in the process of restoring. They welcomed us heartily, and when Mother struggled to find her way around a dog with a large litter of playful puppies on the crumbling porch, the woman shoved some of her children out of her kitchen. She placed a pot of soup in front of us on the table with a huge stack of bologna sandwiches and a couple of jars of pickles. There were soon about as many children around the table as there were puppies on the porch, and everyone was hungry.

Watching them reach for the food, I admired the mother who, a little embarrassed, took the empty plate to make more sandwiches for us. She placed a bowl with fruit on the table telling the children they had to wait for a second helping.

We did not stay very long and once in the car, Mother said, "Those kids wolfed the food down, eating it with the fist. Is that American Style?" It was useless to explain that our children were eating bread without a knife and a fork and I kept quiet.

Mother's critical mood changed quickly when she met her grandchildren. "Amy, your children are so well dressed. They are beautiful," she said.

The four older children crowded around their Grandma, who had brought a present for each one. Naming them from the older to Peter, she said, "Kathy, this is for you; Anne, you were always so tiny. Now you are a big girl, and Janie, do you talk a little Dutch yet? Now, Peter, I brought you a big mug with a picture of a dog, because you are a boy."

She immediately won the trust and love of our children for the six months they stayed. At the smallest cut or scrape, they ran to Beppe, who had discovered M and M candy. With a kiss and a few "happy pills," as she called them, a band-aid was only a minor inconvenience. Mother really spoiled two year old Judy who would immediately let out a howl when she saw the bag with M and Ms!

At first, everything was new to my parents. My father had

a more difficult time adjusting. Mother soon picked up the English from our children, and I was amazed to hear her ask, "Kathy, will you close the window for Beppe?"

Luckily for my father, they found Dutch-speaking friends through a relative in the Netherlands who had asked them to take a small present for him to his Uncle in Grand Rapids. The folks were my parent's age and they liked to take afternoon rides in the country. They entertained my father. He was easily bored and often asked, "Amy, do you have work for me?"

He loved to garden, and our lawn and flower garden has never again looked as neat as when "Pake" took care of it. I had suggested that he bring his wooden shoes, knowing his feet were usually muddy. He was not used to wiping his shoes, and left his dirty "Klompen" at home at the back door.

"Amy," Father scolded," You grow grass in your back yard? With your large family, I must plant beans. It costs a lot to feed us all."

"But, Heit, we need a grassy area for our children to play." I remembered our family joke that Father planted beans anywhere. "Beans grow everywhere in the world, in the Arctic as well as the Tropics. People who are ambitious enough to work the soil will never have to go hungry." I had heard him say it so many times, and it was good it reminded me again.

"Heit, why don't you stake out a garden," I said to please him.

I watched him happily turn the soil. Finding a small rock, he threw it carelessly across the fence into a neighbor's yard. I planned to tell him that it would make more sense to throw them in a pail. Walking out, I heard my neighbor holler, "Get out of my yard, man!"

Father stood his ground and walked out on the soggy lawn. His feet were firmly planted on the freshly seeded soil that had already sprouted a young green carpet of grass.

"You stupid Dutchman! Stop, get out!"

"Yeah, Yeah, Ik Hollander." Slapping his chest, Father stepped up to the new neighbor who angrily using a few choice words shouted, "You dumb old man. Go home!"

With his ever present cigar, Father pointed back to our house. He said, "Yeah, ik Pake..."

"Heit, come here. You are trampling all over the neighbor's new lawn. He is watering his new grass," I said.

Looking at his muddy wooden shoes sinking deep into the fresh dirt, he told me, "Don't worry, Amy. I will leave them at your back door." He did not understand and I apologized for my father who could not understand him. "Keep him home!" the man shouted.

"Come, Amy. That man is worried about me. He should plant beans in that garden. That's what I went over to tell him. Americans are wasteful with good soil," he said.

I agreed with his philosophy, "You made tracks in his beautiful lawn," I said. It didn't make any difference to him. For years, he left his mark on most of the good earth.

Impatiently, he checked our garden, waiting for the little crooked necks of beans to appear. When they did, his reaction was that of a child's wonder. "I've planted a garden and I'm growing beans in America," he said.

With the help of our children, he landscaped the back yard. They transplanted wild flowers from the "Indian Trail" and made a rock garden and a patio from the stones found in the gravel pit.

Claude fabricated a picnic table from scrap lumber and that summer we often ate our lunch under the black ash trees left growing near the abandoned railroad tracks.

At every opportunity, Father took full credit and bragged about his accomplishments. When Claude came home from work, he was first to tell him about it. Claude patiently listened to him, but I became irritated. Claude and I never had a chance to talk since he constantly asked for attention.

"Heit, please leave us alone for awhile," I begged.

"So, you have secrets that I may not know?" he asked once. I had to call him Heit. When I slipped and called him Dad, he said, "Don't pretend you are an American, Amy. We are still Frisians."

Claude is a good listener, and when, hoping for some privacy, I told him we should escape to a "Lover's Lane" near the gravel pit and talk, he happily agreed. I first cried; then we hugged and could laugh again at the small annoyances of coping with our parents for all those months.

The grass was not growing fast enough to keep my father busy. So we bought him a fishing rod and reel for Father's day. Nearby was the old gypsum quarry with little sunfish. Clip-clopping in his wooden shoes on the cement sidewalk, he had a string of youngsters following. They fought to hold his worm can, jabbering in a language he didn't want to learn. He spoke Dutch, his cigar between his lips. As a child, I had often wondered why it didn't fall from his mouth.

It didn't take long and the children were scattered again in our yard. "Pake", my father, patiently fished for hours and came home with a string of three-to four-inch small sunfish. He invariably threw the rod to me. "Amy, please untangle this mess for me while I clean the fish." Used to fishing with a cane pole, he was very impatient with the "new fangled contraption," which was, at the same time, a nuisance and his pride and joy.

One afternoon, I was surprised to see him home so quickly. A cheering group of neighbor kids grouped around him and shouted, "Pake has caught a great big fish. It's a monster fish!"

"Yeah, we have to show this to your mother. This was a fighter, Amy. He pulled like a horse. Today I caught a fish that will give us a meal or two. This fish must weigh over ten pounds!"

I stared in disbelief at the largest carp ever and took a deep breath, "Heit, we cannot eat this fish. It is bony and has a very muddy taste."

I watched my father shrink. He was an elderly man with a crushed ego who had wanted so much to please me. Oh, I loved him, but...

"Pake, you could put a carp under a rosebush for fertilizer," Anne said. She thought she had found the solution.

That finally registered with him. "A rosebush? No, Amy, this fish is so pretty."

"Heit, this is a real catch. Here they call it a sport fish! I will take a picture of you and the fish and you show that to Uncle John, your fishing buddy. He has never caught one like it at home," I said.

He agreed, "It is so beautiful a fish! Amy, will you take me in your car to the quarry and we'll let it go again?"

I had him hold the fish at arm's length so it would look larger and snapped a picture. We then rushed the few blocks to the small man-made lake. He carefully massaged the fish, moving it back and forth until the gills began to pump new life into its body and the carp swam to the deeper water.

My father sighed and said, "I guess this calls for lighting a fresh cigar, Amy."

Pake and the Carp
My Father with Monster Fish

Mother kept busy helping me with the mending and doing the dishes. For my father, it was more difficult. He would take long walks, but when I heard the children say, "No, Pake, don't do that. Mom won't like that," I came running.

Father was neatly slicing squares of sod in the front lawn, planning to work the soil. "Hi, Amy. I have a few beans left and thought to make you a little garden along your driveway."

He was so cheerful, I compromised with his plans. "Heit, the other day I had an idea for a little garden there too. Don't you think a few geraniums and petunias would look pretty? Would you come with me to buy some plants right now?" I asked.

The plants never bloomed. They were destined to catch basketballs, footballs, all the balls thrown by all the kids in the neighborhood. They never had a chance to grow.

Once a week, we stuffed five children, my parents and I into the Studebaker and drove to Olin Lakes where Father fished. The children swam and my mother sat in the shade with her embroidery. She could never understand why we liked to fish, accusing us of double murders, first killing a worm and then a fish. She would not eat fish we had caught.

Mother was a large woman who moved slowly. The children pulled Beppe, huffing and puffing up a sand hill to see "something very beautiful." Soon she stood eye to eye with a huge four-foot long Blue Racer snake sunning in the warm sand. She was a great sport. Hating the sight of even small snakes, she told them, "I have never seen anything so special in all my life." She would have even kissed it had they asked her. She did anything to please her grandchildren.

On our return trip, we stopped for a five-cent ice cream cone if there was no complaining or squabbles in the car. Packed as we were in that small sedan, it was an art to lick a runny melting ice cream cone before picking Claude up from work at his shop.

When school started that fall, Pake missed his little companions. During the day, our back yard was deserted and I found him sitting at the picnic table with a calendar in front of him. He had a cigar box where he kept his money.

"Are you counting your money?" I asked.

"Oh, I've come here with one hundred dollars and now I have one hundred fourteen. The neighbors pay me a few dollars for mowing the lawn and you and Ralph, your brother, do too."

I remembered how frugal and miserly he could be, but he said sadly, "I am counting days too. Don't tell Mother. She loves it here. Well, I better go fishing."

I heard the clip-clopping of his wooden shoes. I missed the happy ring. He was like a carp out of water.

A week before we brought our parents to the train leaving for New York, I told Mother that we were expecting a new baby in March. She did not say, "How nice." Instead she said, "I thought so and I don't ever have to worry about you, because Claude is a wonderful, loving husband."

It was a typical Frisian woman's response, a way of saying, "I love you. You must be happy and grateful for a fine family."

"Well, Ymerke, we are going home!" my father said. It was all that mattered to him now. At the depot, he recognized some of his former companions from the ship who had arrived with him in April. Holding a fishing rod and reel between their knees, the two men waited for their wives to hug the loved ones they were leaving behind.

Father settled next to them and said, "So, you got a new fishing pole too?"

"Yeah, for Father's day," the men said.

"I, too. Are you happy to go home?"

"We sure are. It's been good to see the children, but for us, there wasn't much to do here," one said.

"Yeah, for the wife, it's no problem. For them it is the same as at home, kids! And they always have something in their hands." His friends nodded thoughtfully.

"You are right. It is the language too. And at home in our town, everyone knows me. Here they don't know that I am Baker Hoekstra," my father said.

"That's it!" the men agreed. The three men with fishing poles looked so much alike, all having lost their pride and identity.

As Mother kissed her grandchildren, she counted into their hands an equal number of "Happy Pills," once more. I guessed she was healing the hurt of her own heart.

She said, "I would not mind living in a nice little house right here in Grandville, Amy."

It was not easy for my mother to give her approval, but I knew of her deep love for our family. It was comforting.

Our Extended Family

*B*irds were singing, our neighbors were raking the leaves and children played ball in our back yard. On a beautiful spring day, the Saturday before Easter Sunday, I felt like a queen when Claude brought me home from the hospital with a tiny five pound baby in my arms.

Our Ellie had been the pride of the nurses on the maternity floor. they dressed her in a pretty pink gown, placing her near the window of the nursery. We named her Eleanor Joan after my Tante Aaltje who I loved like a mother.

At nine months, she was running, climbing and tumbling through her first year as if she knew she was to stay ahead of her baby sister who arrived fourteen months later.

She didn't have to worry, Amy June took life much more easily. She was fat, cuddly, smiling and everyone wanted to pinch her rosy cheeks. Claude had named her after me. We had not thought of a name for her thinking that she might have been another boy. He told the nurse, "We now have six beautiful girls and

Kathy, Anne, Janie, Peter, Judy, Ellie, Amy

147

she should have her mother's name." When the nurse came to tell me, I was very pleased and quickly added June, a middle initial for the month she was born.

At times it caused confusion when she was a teenager and boys phoned to speak to Amy, then discovering they possibly had made a date with her mother.

In the same year we also applied for United States citizenship, Claude in the process of filing our papers asked, "Amy, what is your middle initial?"

"I don't have one. My offical name is still Ymkje," I said.

He snickered when signing the forms and sealed the large manila envelope. Several months passed before we were asked to appear at the Fifth District Court of Western Michigan in Grand Rapids for the examination and the swearing in ceremony, pledging allegiance to our new country, the United States of America.

Each individual was asked to come forward. "Amy Joy Van Ooyen?" the judge asked. Shocked by hearing my new name, I stood up, forgetting to raise my hand, then turned to Claude behind me and said for all to hear, "Claude, did you do that?"

The stern judge banged his hammer and spoke loudly now, "Amy Joy Van Ooyen, will you raise your right hand?"

It was now dead still when I answered, "Yes, your Honor," and raised my left hand.

With another bang of the hammer he said, "Amy Joy Van Ooyen, I asked you to raise your right hand!"

I finally got it right and would have raised both hands to be a naturalized citizen of the United States. My stupid performance didn't take away from the joy I experienced when proudly signing my naturalization document Amy J. Van Ooyen. My signature will emphasize the J for the meaning behind my middle name.

During the summer of 1958, Claude took his first week of vacation. Taking two babies camping was impossible and renting a cottage too costly. So we decided to pretend that our house was a vacation home.

I hired someone to do the daily mountain of laundry and we changed the clock one hour ahead for personal day light saving time. Our meals were camp food served from a can. We ate pork and beans, Spam, canned spaghetti, hot dogs and bags full of chips and marshmallows. The kids loved to make biscuits on a stick above glowing coals of our campfire. Mixing water with Bisquick flour to a thick paste, they patted the dough around the top of a stick, roasting it to light brown biscuit. It easily pulls off and one may fill the hole with butter and brown sugar as they preferred.

We explored lakes and sanctuaries when all the neighbors were still getting up. At one wild flower sanctuary which was left natural and untouched, I stepped on a rotten log disturbing a nest of hornets. I was carrying Amy in my arms and she was stung horribly by the cloud of mad insects as were Claude and the rest of our children. We have never again visited the wilds near Lola Lake on future trips to Bikely cottage driving down M 37. Passing the sign, someone would remark, "Remember when we were stung!" We learned to respect nature. I have heard it said, "We came to tame the forest, but it tamed us."

When Judy started kindergarten in the fall of 1959, I realized that with seven children, my hope for continuing nurses' training here in the United States was impossible. There was no other choice than to be a full time Mom.

On Sunday mornings, we all went to church. With the babies in the nursery, I sometimes relaxed too much, dozing off and nodding a full approval to what the then aged pastor said. One exception, a particular topic chosen from the "Lord's Prayer" caught my attention. He spoke about "Give us this day our daily bread!" He did say that it meant not just food but all the blessings of a happy family, health, loved, our home with its conveniences and much more.

After church, Claude and I had an hour to ourselves with a cup of coffee. Undisturbed by the older children and the babies taking a nap, we talked about the pastor's sermon. Claude said, "In the eight years since we've arrived in America with four children, little money and unable to speak a word of English, we've been more than blessed."

I agreed and after preparing a plentiful Sunday dinner, hearing Claude give thanks for the food, the simple request for bread seemed unnecessary.

149

After dinners the girls squabbled about doing the dishes and I heard Claude say, "No arguing now; don't complain. Be happy you have a dirty plate to wash. Many people in the world..."

"We know Dad, you've told us so a thousand times."

I smiled when grumbling, they cleaned the sink.

Claude usually worked long hours during the week but on Saturday he came home earlier. When the paper arrived, I laid it near his chair and an article on the front page got my attention. "A family in Grand Rapids adopts a little girl from Korea," the headline read. The lengthy article explained the plight of mixed race children in Korea, especially girls. A family named Zylstra had, through the work of Harry Holt in Creswell, Oregon , who himself adopted eight children, received this child.

Claude and I had asked at one time if we could help a deprived child and give it a home. Since we were richly blessed, having immigrated to a free country, one more child in our situation, would not make much of a difference. But then I wondered if it would be fair to Claude. He worked many hours.

Making a pot of coffee and taking a quick glance in the mirror before welcoming him home, I told the children, "Dad is coming soon." They usually run down to the corner of Cheyenne drive to greet him and catch a ride in the old station wagon. The chattering group soon dispersed with kids playing in our yard.

Claude, smelling the fresh brewed coffee, sank in his chair and settled down to read the paper. I watched him through the serving window in the kitchen thinking, he looks young yet for forty six. Taking the coffee to him, he in turn said, "You look great, Amy."

"Probably because it is Saturday afternoon and I feel work is finished for another week," I told him.

As if he had read my thoughts, he looked up from the paper and said, "Those children need a home. Have you seen this picture. Maybe we should adopt one."

"Claude, is that fair to you. At almost forty-six, you work long hours," I said.

"What about you? I enjoy my work. There is always a new challenge.

His answer now assured me; it had been good to come to the United States where my husband had all the opportunities to use his talents.

"Well, I might go to the Zylstra family for more information. We don't need to make a decision now," Claude said.

Peter Zylstra gave Claude the address of the Holt Adoption agency. When he heard we had seven children, he told Claude, "Man, I think you are crazy. We have three boys and lost a baby girl. She is not replaceable, but we do love this little tyke too."

At the Holt agency, they may have thought we were insane also. The letter of inquiry was very poorly written and had probably given an unfavorable impression. We wrote another note and a quick reply gave us the answer. We hadn't been far from the truth, "Have you been naturalized, if so please state the facts with a full documentation."

Ouch! In the return mail we made it clear that we were United States citizens. By return mail we received the required forms with a blank page enclosed except for the heading, "Statement of Faith."

Harry Holt, a devout Christian, believed that parents planning to adopt a child from halfway around the world and of a different race were to depend on God for raising such a child.

For us to express our faith in God was impossible. We were not that vocal about our belief and inadequately expressed ourselves in the English language. Claude answered all the questions on the form as well as he could and then left the blank page to me. It was not an easy challenge until I thought of copying the Apostles Creed from the pages of our hymn book.

In perfectly spelled words with good grammar, the common belief confessed through the ages, was actually a cop out. We did not hear from the Holt agency again.

Another summer went by and on a quiet evening walk, Claude and I discussed our disappointment with the agency. "I've heard there are some children who are handicapped, not many families like to adopt them," Claude said.

"Maybe God doesn't want us to have more children and I am not sure I can cope with a slow learning child with all of our lively bunch," I said.

"What about a physical problem? They need a home too," Claude was not giving up on me.

I agreed and he suggested we pray about it. Having come to a decision we again sent a letter to the Holt agency with the information that we were willing to accept a physically handicapped child.

We had not expected an immediate response and were surprised to receive a mimeographed news letter asking for prayer. One request was for a little baby boy, Victor Lee. He was two months old, and had a paralyzed arm caused by a difficult birth.

There was no doubt in my mind. This baby was meant for us. But I, who would be his Mother, did not want him! Definitely not a baby at all, and especially not a handicapped child.

Fighting the thought, I put my two young children in bed for a nap. Since it was Friday, I was scrubbing the kitchen floor. The harder I scrubbed, the worse I began to feel, hating the fact of caring for a handicapped child. I knew it was wrong. On my knees on the floor, I wrestled with God asking for peace of mind. Yet, I stubbornly wished for a way out. Claude is so resourceful, he'll invent a contraption to exercise the muscles in that arm. As a nurse I knew the function of the radial nerve that the doctor said was damaged.

But I found no relief because I had figured it all out and told God what to do; that's what I had done life long and He had blessed me. This time, groping and miserably asking for help, there was not relief.

I scrubbed the dirty breezeway floor and finally realized my own selfishness. It was then that God told me, "Amy, why don't you trust me?"

With a simple answer, "Yes, I will trust you," there was peace. For the rest of my life, in many difficult situations, I learned to trust God.

Showing Claude the newsletter, I asked him, "How do you feel about his little guy who needs a family?"

"It looks like this baby Victor will be a perfect child for us," he said.

"Should we call the agency tomorrow?"

"No, we'll wait and make our decision next week." That seemed overly cautions to me but God already had planned, making the decision for us.

On Monday morning, another letter arrived in the mail and opening it, our phone rang. Claude had a habit of calling at noon. With the envelope in one hand, and the other holding the phone, a small baby picture fell out. "Claude, we've a letter from the Holt agency. Enclosed is a picture of the little boy, Victor Lee," I said.

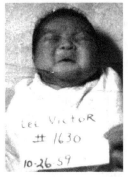

Calvin

"Our letters must have crossed in the mail."

Claude calmly accepting that we were soon to be parents of another son, said, "Why don't you call the Holts now. I'm sure he is the one meant for us."

A steady flow of forms and affidavits explaining his handicap were to be signed. At that time foreign adoptions were by proxy which meant, once the child arrived in the States, he was legally ours. The immigration service making an investigation of the adoptive family was enough to assure the Korean government that the child was well cared for.

Nervous about the thought of having an officer inspect our home, I went on a frenzy of house cleaning. The older children, with their school projects, hobbies, and pets, complained and squabbled. As they cleaned their white mice cages and the aquarium, the hamster escaped and sought shelter under the refrigerator. I had them clean under their beds where I found out they had been hiding their treasures.

Claude stayed calm until I told him to clean up the mess in the basement workshop. "Amy, please, this is a family, not a retirement home. And don't you dare toss anything out!" I was not so sure he had any need for all of his junk.

Dressed in my very best, long before the appointed time the officer was to arrive, I waited for the doorbell to ring. I opened the door to an immaculately dressed person who asked, very friendly, "Are you Mrs. Van Ooyen?"

"Yes," I said and could hardly keep form laughing. He had probably been eating a hot dog for lunch and on his beautiful dark tie sparkled a bright yellow glob of mustard.

Our Ellie woke and dribbled in the living room. He took her in his arms asking me, "You and your husband must like children. I have quite the file on you."

"Oh, yes," I said, happily keeping my eyes on the bright yellow spot of mustard.

"Well, I guess we will add one more. It is then number eight?" he asked.

It took four months before our son from Korea arrived on the 14th of April, 1960. They were tense weeks. Mr. Holt had informed us that many of the orphan babies died of what he called, "Mother sickness," a lack of love.

I flew with another expectant mother to Portland Oregon where many parents were anxiously waiting, comparing pictures. Each had their own story to tell. When finally the airline prop jet plane from Korea landed with sixty-nine children on board, accompanied by attendants and a doctor, we were told it had been a fast trip of nineteen hours.

The older children, confused and tired, were first down the ramp and quickly caught in the arms of loving parents. It reminded me of our family and the anxiety of coming to a new world.

The babies were carried down in white carton boxes, each one with their Korean name and that of the adopted family. When finally the last box had been placed in a large room, I had not recognized our name which is often mispronounced. "Mrs. Van Ye, is Mrs. Van Ye present?" I heard a lady call, hearing the"Van" was enough. I took a fat little boy in my arms. His face was covered with infected chicken pox but he smiled happily when I gave him his bottle. He took it greedily with both hands, using his right hand which was supposed to be paralyzed, as well as his left.

"He is not paralyzed," I said to my friend who was cuddling her beautiful two year old daughter.

She was too busy to answer me. With tears streaming down my cheeks, I contacted the social worker, trying to tell her of the healing of my baby's arm. She was too busy also. I walked up to Mr. Holt with Calvin stretching his full tummy He smiled, displaying a bare belly with a huge umbilical hernia. Mr. Holt, annoyed with another hysterical mother, pointed to the bay's navel and said, "Put a silver dollar on that and it will heal quickly."

At last I found a listening ear when I called Claude. "Our baby is all right. His arm has healed. He has chicken pox but he is just fine," I said. "I will soon be home. When you take the children to the airport, have them wear the clothes which I've laid out for you. Please, they must look nice."

We stayed overnight with friends who were not in a hurry to take us to the airport. The plane had left without us. Rescheduling again meant a night flight to Chicago and a disappointment for Claude and our children. Calvin slept soundly in my arms and I began to feel very tired. A passenger in the seat next to me asked several questions and offered, "May I hold him for awhile?"

"But your navy blue suit, what will your wife say when you get home? This flannel blanket is brand new and he is all infected with chicken pox," I said.

"I will have to do some explaining to my wife. Maybe when I tell her of holding a little Korean baby in my arms, we will also adopt," he said.

"Don't take him home," I said before taking a quick nap.

Arriving at the O'Hare airport, the person thanked me for the privilege of trusting him with our new baby. I am almost sure he also became an adoptive parent.

Again we missed our connection and late in the afternoon, we landed at the old Kent County airport where our children were lined up against the fence. Claude took him from me, very happy to have us back home. I looked at the three younger girls and asked Claude, "Why do these kids wear those old clothes and backwards too? The buttons are to fasten in the front. With the collars so tight against the neck, they can't breathe!"

"Well, we've been here now for the third time. First they were dressed in the clothes you laid out. You weren't on the plane and I bought them an ice cream cone. It dripped and messed on all of them. The second time I thought you said the kids should look nice and they were wearing Sunday clothes. They were so disappointed when you didn't arrive that I took them out for a hamburger and orange drink. That was spilled when they had an accident. Again we went home and I put them in playclothes. I don't know the front from back on a shirt. It sure is awful good to have you come home again."

I sure was happy too. Everyone crowded around the bassinet when I changed Calvin's diaper. Judy, pulling herself up to take a good look at her new brother, watched him with an open mouth when Calvin did what comes natural for a little boy. He aimed right at her, a well deserved humiliation for her curiosity. She let out scream of surprise but Peter said, "Good for you, I finally have a brother!"

Although ten years apart, the two were very close. Calvin chose, when he grew up, to sit next to Peter at the table. In church I watched him, trustingly placing his little hand on the knee of his big brother, a gesture that reminded me of trusting God for the many happy and more difficult years ahead.

Calvin
(18 months)

Our Busy Years

*D*uring the summer of 1960, a social worker from the Holt adoption agency, Mrs. Myrtle Croy came to Michigan checking on the well-being of families who had adopted Korean children.

Mrs. Croy told us she had planned to see us in the afternoon. Since we were a large family, I invited her for dinner when Claude was home so she could become acquainted with the entire family.

I prepared a dinner of mashed potatoes, green beans, a salad and nine Salisbury steaks. If the smaller children each had a half one, I figured there would be plenty. As frequently happened, one of the children brought a friend home, and I quickly added an extra table setting.

The children eyed the good food hungrily, and I heard Claude say, "Don't worry. Mom always cooks enough. There is plenty of food for everyone. Now we will all be quiet. I'll ask for a blessing."

Mrs. Croy looked pleased, and I was sure I would make a good impression, first handing our guest the plate with the meat. The phone rang and I hurried to the kitchen. It was a long conversation, too long. Returning to the family room, my family was silent. There was none of the normal chatter and clatter. Anne was sniffing and Jane wiping a tear. Claude sat at the end of the table waiting. I said, "Sorry to have taken so long. Why didn't you begin eating?"

"We are waiting for you to do a miracle," Claude grinned.

"We are short one steak," Anne said. Her big brown eyes glancing at her friend who was the only one enjoying one of the largest steaks. My plate was heaped with a stack of meat.

"There weren't enough this time," Claude said.

"Yes, Daddy gave his steak to you, but now he has

nothing." Jane, trying to hide her tears, ran from the table.

"So, we then gave ours to Daddy, but he did not want it and heaped it all on your plate," Kathy said.

"Yes, I did too!" Mrs. Croy chuckled, amazed by the show of support.

What must she think of all of this? She'll report my flop right to the home office. But she said, "To be a part of our family, I had to join them. I've never seen a more loyal family."

By the time I had divided the meat, chiseling a small part of each steak, Anne's friend had almost emptied her plate, smacking her lips.

From that day on, the social worker was "Auntie Myrtle" to our children and my dear friend. She became so much a part of the family that if it was at all possible, she was present at weddings, Christmas and occasionally came for a summer vacation.

She decided to stay with us overnight and passed her initiation test gallantly. It was not very restful. Kathy and Anne had been collecting insects for a science contest all summer: bugs, butterflies, moths, anything that crawled or had wings. All the family, friends and neighbors were involved. Finding a safe place for the styrofoam board with pinned up creatures was a problem.

Calvin had eaten a few specimens and it created a disaster because some beetles come around only once a year. They blamed me for it, so I hid the collection under a bed in our den, that also served as a guest room.

On Aunt Myrtle's first night at our home, a large green luna moth, which we thought had succumbed in the freezer, resurrected in the dark, as moths will do. With pins and all, it fluttered around Aunt Myrtle's head on the pillow. When the light was turned on, the moth flew to the ceiling. After an unsuccessful chase, she chose to lie down again. And then the reflection of her gray hair attracted the insect again. Not wanting to crush the delicate nymph, she finally caught it in a shear curtain, folding it carefully over a chair. She then discovered a large dragonfly had wriggled itself free from a carton.

In the morning she told me, "I had enough and killed that zooming bug. There must be thousands more of those flying at a nearby pond."

"I'm sorry our home is so buggy this summer," I said, hoping she would not look in our freezer which stored odd things.

That evening Claude told Myrtle, "At the time we applied for Calvin's adoption, we received a double set of forms. We've been thinking of filing for another child."

"Oh no! At the office we thought you already had a large family...well it was a difficult decision. Your letter was not convincing. It was very poorly written," she admitted. "We surely didn't intend for you to adopt two children."

"Don't you feel one little Korean boy at the end of our family may feel lonely?" I asked.

She laughed. "I don't think that is possible, although he may like a little brother."

We sent a request with the second set of forms to the agency and they promptly assigned us a cute little baby boy. On the third of June, 1961, I traveled, by train, with three companions to Portland Oregon. When Alvin Lee arrived, he was a very sick six-month-old baby, but a fighter. He coughed and wheezed, and I soon realized he probably had pneumonia.

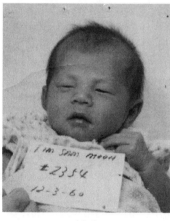
Alvin

On the return trip, two physicians came to the Denver train depot. Examining him, they gave Alvin an injection and upon our arrival in Grand Rapids, he was hospitalized. It took a week before we could take him home. Now Calvin had a little brother named Alvin. And they tell me to this day they don't know who is named Calvin or Alvin because "Mom in one breath called us Calvin and Alvin!"

With nine children, steak was not on the menu. I had more tricks for a balanced budget and diet than many authors in a "How to Do" book wrote about.

Turkey legs with a little imagination were priceless. And hamburger will stretch to a wholesome meal adulterated with stale homemade bread and a few eggs. Potatoes are a staple, and I bought carrots and onions in twenty-five pound bags.

Mr. Larry Seeley, our next door neighbor whose mother had eight children offered a good recipe to stretch the budget:

Fill a six quart soup kettle with boiling water. Dice a dozen or more large po- tatoes with 2 pounds of carrots and a half dozen onions. Let it simmer for two hours, then add one pound hamburger and a quart of milk. Season it with salt and pepper to taste. Simmer until dinner time.

Alvin (18 months)

"Now that is a meal that will serve all of us any time," he said.

I added a handful of chopped parsley for garnish and served hamburger soup with several loaves of homemade bread. The children licked the pan clean. For a side dish, I gave each one a bowl of applesauce.

We had few doctor's bills. The children were very healthy, but there were the bills from doctor "Pain" our dentist, that had me worried.

"Doctor Pain" was very reasonable, but he did not believe in novacain injec- tions, telling his patients the prick hurts more than a slight sensation from his drill.

In his waiting room, patients were soothing their nerves by reading his volumes of comic strips pasted in an al- bum. There were two choices, "Born too Soon" and "Orphan Annie."

Children vented their anxiety by toss- ing red rubber canning rings, already out of use at that time, unto hooks on his of-

Alvin and Calvin

fice door. It was not difficult to imagine that they actually were projectiles aimed at their tormentor's crooked nose.

"You're first, Mom. You have to go first," the kids told me when Doctor "Pain" appeared to face our tribe. He was probably more worried than I was, fearing the hurt of an empty check book.

Promising the group to be first in the chair actually was a psychological move. I told them, "When you hear the slightest little peep from me, I'll treat you to an ice cream cone; and when you don't cry, we will all have a chocolate sundae at the Payne's drugstore." This was actually the real name of the pharmacy on main street.

The kids were quiet, listening through a crack in the door. The dentist happily praised our "well-behaved" children. Tallying our bill, he counted the children's names listed from the oldest to Alvin, the youngest. He didn't keep records on each child, but mercifully gave a discount saying, "Oh, those were only surface problems, only little pinholes, Mrs. Van Ooyen."

We then dashed off to the drugstore; but I was left with the bill and only a few weeks before school started. There were the usual expenses of shoes and school clothes. By September, we were broke and the dentist bill for one hundred and fifty dollars was half of Claude's weekly paycheck. My pride was involved. Grandville is only a small town, and my family was very visible. We must at all cost save our reputation.

I worried, finding little comfort in reading verses like, "Remember the birds of the air and the lilies of the field. They spin not and yet... King Solomon was not dressed like them!" A lot of cavities to pay for is not like buying beautiful clothes, I told God! I grumbled a lot to Claude, and he was the one who came up with the solution.

The apple harvest was delayed after a cool summer, and the Mexican fruit pickers moved on to another area. With a shortage of workers, the fruit growers were desperate for apple pickers. We picked apples on five Saturdays for twenty-five cents a bushel during September and part of October. The weather was sunny and we brought bushels of "drops" home, which are usually riper and sweeter. We paid "Doctor Pain" in full! Until this day I have a clear memory of bright red apples sitting in the dentist chair.

Our children too remember that fall when many jars of applesauce lined up on the shelves in our basement. Judy, coming home from school to the kitchen, told me, "Mmmm! Smells good here, Mom, and you are so smart."

"Oh, yes," I smiled, thinking she complimented me for canning more applesauce.

"Yes, you are, you are smart!"

"Well?" I asked, not sure what she was wanting from me.

"Do you remember when you gave me a permission slip to attend the hygiene class in school?"

"Hmm, yeah, what about it?" I had almost forgotten. The apples were a treasure!

"Well, it was like you told me, Mom. You know everything. Today the nurse came to school and it was all like you said about the Administration of girls."

She ran upstairs shouting, "And I told the nurse I knew already about it. Mom had told me everything!"

"Oh!" I said, surprised that Judy was soon a teenager too and the apples weren't so important now.

Our children were good average students but for a straight "A", I looked at the bottom list of subjects on their report for music and art. They had inherited their creativity from Claude. The rest were "B's" and "C's" mostly.

Our piano, that we bought for eleven dollars never became a favorite instrument for them to play. It gave only the basics for music. Each one chose an instrument of their choice: flutes, violins, a cello, a clarinet and a horn and for Calvin who didn't have a musical ear, the drums.

At the end of the school year, Claude and I were to divide our loyalties, attending many concerts of the high school, junior high and the younger children from grade six to kindergarten.

Before Dad came home after work at six p.m., our house was a racket with young musicians practicing on flutes, squeaking violins, brass instruments and the beat of drums. Every half hour, one child took his turn banging on the piano while I prepared a meal in the kitchen.

Only faintly hearing the doorbell ring, I met with a neatly dressed man and thought he must be selling magazines or burial plots. They always came along at dinnertime. Our community was developing so quickly that two new cemeteries were competing for selling lots as fast as the contractors were building homes.

"Are you selling grave sites?" I asked the perplexed man in front of me.

"Ma'am, I actually do, for the Pine Restviews Gardens."

"Oh, we aren't interested right now, sir," and I wanted to close the door on him.

He kept his foot between the door. "I agree, you should not make plans for your funeral yet. There is a lot going on here," he said.

The dissonance of the drum and instruments were embarrassingly noisy. He explained that he played the flute in the Grand Rapids Symphony and asked, "May I come in? Maybe I can give a few pointers." I thought the man was too polite for a very persistent salesman and he probably was a very talented musician. He talked and listened to the children play, forgetting his purpose of selling, but I thought he had been right. We were not in the market for a burial plot yet. We lived to make music.

Sunday afternoons, Claude took several children for walks out in the fields behind our home. They always returned with treasures for me. Later in the evening, everyone gathered around the piano for a family concert. Sometimes the neighbors came in the yard to listen when they heard the music through the open windows. For a final number on the program, Claude led them in the hymn:

> *For all the saints who from their labors rest*
> *who those by faith...*
> *before the Lord confessed.*
> *Thy name of Jesus, be forever blest*
> *Hallelujah! Hallelujah!*

The loudly played Hallelujahs had not quite finished echoing from our large family room walls when everyone sat down at the table for a well deserved lunch.

The harmony in our family could at times turn quickly to annoying discords.

"What happened here?" Claude asked. He noticed one of my shoes stuck in a broken pane of the kitchen window. Surprised by the sullen group when he returned home from work, he looked for an explanation from me.

"Mom got mad," Ellie said.

"She threw a shoe at us, but I ducked. She missed," said Alvin.

"Were you fighting? Claude asked.

"Of course they were. I am sick and tired of you kids. There was no reason for you to argue. Go sit at the table. Dad is home." I scowled from one to another.

Claude was tired, and I wished I had given him a better welcome home. We ate in record time, silently brooding about the shoe stuck between the window panes. The dishes were finished quickly and the towels neatly hung on the bar. There was none of the usual fooling around with arguments about who would wash, dry, or clean up.

On the night before, Claude and I had scrubbed two bushels of carrots a friend gave to us. I was cutting and cooking carrots before the family was up in the morning, imagining the jars brightening the display on the shelves in the basement, along with green beans and applesauce.

By the time the children were about ready to come home from school, eighteen two quart-size jars were cooling on a cabinet in the kitchen.

Running quickly to town for an errand, I was delayed and came home to a kitchen floor covered with a thick layer of bright orange carrots and broken glass jars. All I saw was orange. "I wanted to leave the mess for you to see!" I told Claude.

"That's why you threw the shoe at the kids?"

"No, I didn't then. It was a sight, almost comical, five grade school kids with nothing to say, staring at a pile of cooked carrots. I told them to scoop the mess into a pail and throw it in the compost. They didn't move until I began to laugh and said, "Use the dust pan and mop the floor. Be careful you don't cut yourself on the glass." It was so funny I left them to finish the dirty job and read the newspaper in the family room. And then I heard those kids bicker about whose fault it was and calling each other names. That's when I got really mad and threw my shoe at them."

Claude, picturing the situation asked, "Who spilled those carrots?" And then he began to snicker.

"You come home and it's all cleaned up! It's report card day. Alvin had a "D" for math and Ellie told him nobody in our family had ever gotten a "D". She scolded him, and to prove she was right, she balanced on that free standing cabinet to reach for a box on the top shelf where I've saved the kid's report cards for years. She and the whole kaboodle fell, every jar smashed on the floor. I don't ever want to cook a carrot again!"

For some time there was not much arguing at our home, because Claude told the children, "I'm not going to fix that window. Understand why?" One glance at the broken window was enough to end temper flare ups and disagreements in the family.

Dinner time was often hectic with school children telling their various experiences. The younger kids did not have much of a chance to speak up, but they took full advantage of their turn to pray. Their prayers lengthened by mentioning everyone around the table by name. They extended it across the ocean to grandparents, the church, and the neighbor's dog Cindy. The younger the child, the longer his prayer, with the older children warning the devout petitioner by coughing. If it took too long, there was a kick under the table.

Calvin prayed very slowly. He thought a long time, trying to say it right. At his turn, someone would say, "Cal, please, hurry up this time!" "Hmm," Cal began, clearing his throat, I "Hmm. . . Lord. . . thank you. . . for this food. . . hmm, hmm. . .and for Mom. . . that she. . . cooked. . . We know hmm, it really comes from you! Hmm. . . because. . . like I saw. . . this morning a robin and, hmm. . . and it was like you said, you feed the birds . . . and I saw this robin. . . and he pulled and pulled this big. . . fat worm. . . ."

"Oh, yuck, Cal! Mom, stop him," one of the finicky teenage girls shouted. "Quit, Cal! Mom, make him quit!"

"Amen! It's time to eat, a very good prayer Calvin."

Claude complimented him and calmly filled his plate.

Calvin proudly looked around at his family, until I dished up the food for the smaller children. Again, we had heard from the mouth of little children that we were blessed.

I usually cooked the general fare and didn't make exceptions for the individual's taste. The ones who complained had to take their food to the basement stairs. It was amazing how quickly they returned with an empty plate. It wasn't until years later that I learned their secret. Our sump pump hole had been fed several portions of peas and spinach through the years.

Our children attended a parochial school, and the tuition began taking a large bite out of our budget. For several years, the tax return and Claude's two-week vacation pay brought it back into balance. Through a friend, we rented a cottage at Bitely Lake for twenty-five dollars. Bob Goudsward's generous offer came exactly when we needed it most.

The older children canoed, hiked, swam and sunbathed on the dock. The three teenage girls attracted the older fishermen on the lake. It couldn't possibly be their favorite fishing hole. I expect they admired the long tan legs and firm bodies diving and somersaulting from the raft. Teenage guys raced past in speedboats, leaving a silver spray and a wake that left the girls squealing until one fellow picked up our Kathy. She talked him into taking her sisters for a ride too. The two made long evening walks to Bitely and the only general store where he bought her an ice cream cone for a treat or a coke and chips.

Claude joined us on weekends. He didn't complain about working the daily grind when we had fun. But it was twice as much fun when we all went blueberry picking and he rowed the boat or tippy canoe. Every year, he came up with one of his new inventions. First we brought a sailboat made of rubber inner tubes. The thing seemed to fear setting out on the lake but came steadily back to shore. No matter what wind direction, it landed safely at our dock.

The next one was for the four younger children. He tied bike tires to aluminum floats we had found at the shore of Lake Michigan. The handy life preserver worked well. It was light and never got soggy. They soon learned to swim, looking like small torpedoes with metal casings.

He was sure his last crazy invention would be a great attraction called a "Leap Frog." One had to stand on the rear of a double board resembling a giant clothes pin, hop up and down and leap much like an amphibian across the surface of the lake. He and the girls tried it, but after a few spurts, the thing sinks as it loses speed.

Our cottage at Bitely is where ten years of memories are stored. We know the secrets of the Manistee forest, its trout streams, dark spooky places like "Devil's Lake", the area where wild turkeys gobble noisily, and we left behind the grave of our pet raccoon, Rocky who was killed by a speeding car. On the west side of the cottage, a sign marks where he is buried. It cost nearly a whole box of band aids to carve Rocky's name and date of departure on a slab of hardwood, but it was soothing to the grieving process.

The last summer our family was at Bitely Lake we faced a large increase in school tuition. Nine children were enrolled from grade to high school, and when they brought home a note saying they needed a school bus driver for a morning and evening route, I applied.

Surprisingly, I got the job, and earned a large part of the tuition. I had nightmares about kids crossing in front of the bus or cars that didn't stop for the red signal warning lights. Several of the mothers worried too. Leaving their children to a woman driver wasn't heard of in our conservative little town. This was a first, and I was accused of zig-zagging down the country roads, which may have some truth to it.

My former colleague, who knew the most rowdy and naughty kids, left them for me to pick up. They threw hats from the open windows, and I refused to stop and find them. They brought snakes on the bus to scare girls, and apple cores flew past my head. They tried to show me how tough and sexy seventh and eighth graders are by taking apart Playboy magazines and taping the naked exposures to the ceiling of my bus. After returning from filing a gas slip in the office, the bus with little brats waited expect-

The Grandville Schoolbus

antly for my reaction. I certainly was not going to give them the satisfaction of taking those down.

"Well, we'll go home now to show your Mom. She likes to see beautiful girls too, " I said as I calmly took my place at the wheel.

"We're only kidding, Mrs. Van," one of the naughtiest boys said.

"He found them in his father's shop, in a drawer," his friend said, snickering and pulling a centerfold from the ceiling. Knowing the family well, the old yellow Playboys must have been a secret skeleton in his father's closet.

My bus driving for one-seventy-five per hour was more fun than profitable. The kids and their mothers began to trust me. Climbing on board they would greet me singing, "One, two, three, four, five, six, seven, eight! Who do we appreciate? Mrs. Van! Mrs. Van!" And the last day before Christmas vacation they showered me with little presents when in chorus, all the bus load sang, "We wish you a Merry Christmas and a Happy New Year!"

On my first bus trial run, my children already home from school, surprised me with a cup of hot tea and a cookie. "You always did this for us. Now it's your turn, Mom," Kathy said.

For the last fifteen years of bus driving, I took twenty-two handicapped children to seven different schools in Grand Rapids. I learned sign language from the deaf children. I received passionate hugs in busy traffic from a brain damaged eighteen year old boy who fell in love with me. A blind boy taught me to be grateful. On a dark morning, I asked him, "Mark, why are the deaf kids so very quiet today?"

He answered," Mrs. Van, those kids can't see to talk. I am blind, but I can hear and talk. I'm lucky!"

He observed more than I, but he did not like to sit next to a child who could not hear because he said, "they are always bumping me asking for attention." I found him a seat next to Tom who had been paralyzed since birth and the two fantasized, traveling through space, dreaming up "Star Trek" stories. The two explored the universe without a handicap.

Glen, totally deaf, was my protector. In sign language imitating a police car siren, he warned me to slow down when speed limits changed. Unexpectedly hollering at the top of his voice, he could scare me into stopping.

The longer working hours and better pay were now helping the children through college. They worked hard during the summer months themselves and had scholarships, but money was still tight.

Friends would ask, "What are the girls taking up? Did they go for a Mrs. degree?" Maybe so, but the fellows who called must have been very brave and determined to take the girls out. They had to pass a critical inspection from a family with younger brothers and sisters who volunteered free advice and unsolicited information.

We weren't always sure who was coming to pick up Kathy, Anne or Jane, so one day they told a young man, "If you are here for Anne, she is out with David, and Jane is already gone."

"Oh, she has?" the young man said.

"Yes, but I think she might like you too. Why do you wear girl's shoes?"

He looked at the penny loafers on his feet and said, "Don't you like them? They're in style."

"Well, I think she likes them."

"Does she have more friends?"

"Oh yeah, there is David, John, but I think she likes Don best."

The Last Picture of My Parents With Our Children

The young man's spirit dropped with the kids chanting, "He wears girl's shoes, he wears girl's shoes," trailing behind him as he walked to his parked car.

They were well-acquainted with Jim, Kathy's friend, who regularly came in an old blue Chevy. It amazed me every time when the rusty old car always brought her safely home.

I tried my best to distract the group but made my own mistakes. Jim and Kathy had taken a ride, and near the beach at Lake Michigan Jim picked Kathy a bouquet of wildflowers and showed them to me. "Oh, what beautiful concubines," I said.

"Mom! Those are columbines. Don't say anything if you're not sure!"

"Well, they're pretty," I said and apologized with a smile.

"Can you talk like Donald Duck? Jane's boyfriend, Paul talked like Donald Duck and we like him best. Why don't you try?" Calvin asked a young man.

It left the guy speechless and he never returned. I felt sorry for him, but Claude was not at all. "At least we know the fellows are sincere when they keep coming," he said.

When my parents and Grandma Van Ooyen came to visit

in the summer of 1965, we had thirteen persons around the dinner table. Grandma Van Ooyen stayed with Claude's sister and her family and joined us on weekends.

We rented Bitely cottage for three weeks, which gave me relief, since the older children worked and came for the week-end only.

My father fished from dawn to dark from shore, or at the neighbor's dock. I had given him five dollars, knowing he would finally run out of bait, although he had found three cans of worms with my help. I had hidden one can, hoping to fish myself. When Mother took an afternoon nap and the children were playing, I had one hour free. I looked for the hidden can and it was gone!

"Heit, have you seen my worms?" I asked.

He stood near our dock puffing on his cigar. "Yeah, Amy, I found them. Want a couple?"

I was furious at my Dad. "Those were my worms. I gave you an extra five dollars to buy your own!"

"Oh, I took them. You've much better eyes for picking worms than I," he said.

Knowing how thrifty he was, I asked angrily, "What did you do with the money I gave you?"

Probably overworked, I ran back to the cottage and cried. One hour fishing alone in the boat was all I had hoped for.

He came to me and when there were just the two of us he confessed, "Yemerke, I am sorry, but I. . . well, in the bait shop are smokes too, and I bought cigars with your money."

I forgave him and would now gladly buy my father a life-long supply of worms and cigars. Father died when he was almost ninety-one years old after grieving for my mother for six years. They were reunited in heaven on her birthday.

We met again five years later on their golden anniversary when we made our first return visit to the Netherlands. For the first time, our noisy home was quiet. The younger children, the dog, cat, parakeet and white mice all were visiting friends for two weeks. Claude and I were reunited with our relatives and friends after a nineteen-year absence.

It was then that Claude found an old friend waiting for him

in a small storage place behind his mother's home. Almost two decades had passed since we exchanged his reed organ for a piano on Hall street, but Claude's fingers were trained for the organ, and touching her yellowed keys produced a raspy tone.

Startled by what he heard, he said, "She is in need of care. We must bring her home, Amy." I noticed him caressing her dull cabinet, and I agreed.

One year later, with the children shouting loudly, the old reed organ arrived at our home in the United States, and we were reunited again.

When we chose to live in the forest of the Upper Peninsula of Michigan, the little reed organ went with us. So did Mr. Johann S. Bach; he came too!

Our reed organ found a final home at the Eel Lake cabin where we, with the loons and nature, give thanks for living.

We never had it so good.

"Who are You?"

esterday it happened again. "May I ask you where you're from?"

The friendly waitress, tipping the coffee pot ready to fill my cup, smiled. "You have an accent," she said.

"Oh?"

"Yes, what is your nationality?"

I wanted to say, "I'm an American." But I answered, "Well, I've been living in the States for over forty years, but still talk like 'Diss'! We are Dutch and arrived from Holland in 1951."

"It sounds cute. Don't ever lose that." The coffee splashed in my cup.

Serving her customers at the next table, she asked, "Just a drop yet?"

I watched her hurrying to the kitchen.

We are used to this question. At our home, in the store, at church, anywhere the question comes naturally, politely, bluntly, or out of genuine interest: "Who are you?"

Somewhat defensive, my answer is a smile. "Since 1951, we came...," hoping the person will realize that we have lived in the United States for nearly a half century and yet, we are new transplants who talk "funny."

Be careful, be friendly, be nice. Roots are cautiously probing the foreign soil. We must not crowd those who came before us. Feeling, searching, touching very sensitively, one must not grow too fast. Unnoticed and never towering above those who stand tall, one tries to lean on them, be patient.

The lessons are from experience. Our "seedlings" understand the process well; children are very sensitive.

Kathy and Anne learned it first.

"Mom, you don't have to come to parent teachers conferences. Our grades are good."

The little slips of paper fluttered near the cooking pots on the sink. I read, "Parents-Teachers Conference. Oct. 6th and 7th. School is dismissed at noon."

"Great," I said, stirring a large kettle with applesauce.

"You're busy canning, aren't you?" Anne decided to remind me that my place was in the kitchen.

"Don't bother, Mom." Kathy thought to add a little more pressure.

"It will be fun for Dad and I to talk with your teachers. I am glad you did so well," I said.

"But Mom!"

The two 9th and 10th grade girls looked worried.

"Mom, we do have good grades," Anne hesitated. "But..."

Kathy, a year older, bluntly said, "We don't want you to go Mom."

"Why not?" My suspicion that the grades were not that good for the first six week period made me angry. "Do you hide the truth?"

"Well, you see, Mom. You don't understand," Anne stammered.

Giving me a straight answer, Kathy delivered the punch. "If you come to our school, everyone will know that we are Dutch," she said.

"You talk different, really, Mom." Anne's big brown eyes brimmed, hiding tears.

"I am very proud of you. Daddy and I will tell the teachers so too."

There was not much more to say. I did understand. It is not easy to be good, admitting our parents talk "funny." The old roots are there, trimmed, yes, also constantly probing. The cultivation of trust is a slow process.

Finding an after-school job requires lots of trust.

"Who are you?"

Once I heard it said, "Where there is hope, there is faith." For Kathy, it almost disappeared and changed to frustration. In our small town, relatives and the children of friends found work in the local drugstore or bakery, not just babysitting for fifty cents an hour from 8 p.m. to midnight. The two dollar bills often were one dollar and some change.

"Really, Mom, I did the dishes, picked up everything, and gave the kids a bath."

I believed my daughters and hurt for Kathy.

"They did not need more help, but someone got the job," she explained.

Rejection? Not really, unintentional, the friendly person beginning a conversation, noticing a very good friend, would leave me, gasping for air. I felt like a fool. My roots had not yet firmly taken hold.

Kathy's work permit and her new social security card were still hidden in her purse. I worried with her, and yet, someday, she might be unbelievably tough.

"Mom, I got a job! A real job, at the Grandville Rest Home, every day, two hours after school and all day Saturday."

Before I could congratulate Kathy, Anne snapped, "You better work hard. Next year I want to apply."

One firm root piercing the hard soil, crumbled the last resistance and thrusting deep, made space for the next one, and the next one, then the other, until finally, six beautiful plants thrived in new soil.

One evening we waited at the gate for Kathy who, finishing work, came running to the car. Pausing, she picked a daisy. "Just a moment, Mom." She hurried back, returning quickly. "I gave Mrs. Berg that flower. It makes her happy. She will pick one petal at a time; it will keep her busy for awhile." Hope, with faith, will love.

The Love God Plant

The calendar said spring, but the winter dragged on. Arriving home from my early morning bus route, I found my house empty but cluttered. Our younger children had left for school and the older ones to college in a nearby city. Dirty breakfast dishes were stacked in the sink, a forgotten book laid on the kitchen table. Someone would be calling, "Please, Mom, will you take my math book to school before second hour? I love you!"

Soon the phone rang and I scolded. "Once, only once more, I do this for you. Next time, I don't care if you receive a bad grade."

Stumbling over boots in the porch, I reached the old station wagon and drove to the high school grumbling, "When will they ever grow up?" A March snow squall plastered the windshield, the wipers clogged. My spirits drooping, I arrived home again.

Entering the porch, I noticed the plant. Stunned, I looked at the huge bulging wrapping that could not hold its secret. It had been delivered at my doorstep in the short time I'd left the house. The azalea was almost in full bloom, a gorgeous plant with a large cloud of pure white blossoms.

Thrusting the tip of my finger in the soil, I felt it was in need of water. Spraying it carefully, I found the small accompanying envelope with a card. Typed on it, I read my name and the words "Love, God."

I did not think it strange and wasn't that surprised. Now, where must I place it so everyone who entered our home would notice my perfect gift? I decided on the area leading from the kitchen to the family room. There the plant standing on a small bench displayed all her beauty; but her surroundings began to look rather shabby. Quickly disposing of old magazines, papers, and other undefined clutter of a busy household, I tried to make our home worthy of this special gift from God.

176

Taking a break, I made a fresh cup of coffee and my neighbor came to borrow an egg. "Is it your birthday?" she asked me, noticing the beautiful azalea.

"No, Someone gave it to me," I smugly answered.

Jo is not a very nosy person, so I told her, "Why don't you look at the card?"

"Oh!" she said when she read it and left. It then dawned on me it's not so often that one receives a plant from God. That made me a little uncomfortable, but also happy. I left early in the afternoon to drive my school bus route for twenty-two very handicapped children. Noticing my change in attitude, we had a pleasant two-hour ride.

Returning home, I found the younger children admiring my plant. "Mom, who gave you that flower?" one asked.

"Look at the card," I answered.

"We did, but someone must have ordered that for you," Eleanor quipped. At thirteen, she had quick answers for everything.

Calvin, a few years younger, thoughtfully said, "You earned

it, Mom!"

"Could it be from Dad?" Amy asked.

"No, he wouldn't have enough money," Eleanor wise-cracked. She thought it silly her younger sister would even suggest that.

But Amy seriously answered, "Well, yes, it's almost too nice for us."

They all agreed Dad could never afford the extravagance, although he would bring me flowers on a Sunday afternoon after taking a walk with the children in the field.

I prepared the evening meal for the family, feeling special.

At six o'clock my husband came home. "A gift?" my husband asked when he greeted me. I showed him the card. When he read who the Sender was, he gave me a kiss saying, "That's great, you deserve it," without asking questions.

But the older children had many. "Who gave that plant to you Mom?"

Jane reasoned it was delivered by the local floral shop. She immediately left for town to find out who called in the order.

Peter said, "It is neat. Someone likes you Mom, but he is using God-no fair."

Jane, returning soon and disappointed, told us, "All they said was someone phoned by 'Floral Express' and it's paid for."

The Gift created a festive and lighthearted conversation for our evening meal. The boys, whose turn it was to do the dishes, did so without squabbling about who would wash, dry, or clean up. Even Alvin, lively and quick, tiptoed around the plant.

Judy gave thanks for the azalea during the evening prayer. She mentioned God's helper. "We just don't know who it can be. Mom has no idea, but you must know, God," she said.

I told her I did not care to know.

Everyone admired the beautiful white azalea except one very conservative person. He read the card and turned in disgust. Shaking his head he said, "Fanatics. That's blasphemy. God is not mocked."

One lady, a new convert and happy about her new found faith read the little card and lifted her arms singing, "He is Lord!

Did you praise Him too, did you?"

"No, I didn't, but I said 'thank you'," I answered. She left wondering about my sincerity, and shaking her head.

Then my best friend Alice came for a short visit and we talked over a good cup of coffee.

"It would scare me a little receiving a gift from God," she told me. Then she asked, "Don't you have any idea who gave it? I'd be somewhat uncomfortable. Didn't you have a weird feeling when you opened that envelope and read who the Sender was?"

"Alice, this person may want to say 'thank you' to God, and I'm the recipient. I've no idea who the person is, and I've been grateful for the surprise."

She understood as a good friend would.

The "Love God plant." as the children named the azalea, liked all the attention and flourished until one day, a lady admiring its flowers found the small envelope and read the card. She began to preach a sermon warning me that this Gift, a plant from God is not a ticket to heaven and that it did not make me a saint. "God is not finished with you yet," she told me.

After she left the azalea seemed sad, and so was I. Taking it from the stand, I sprayed its delicate flowers with lukewarm water, and the shine returned to the dark green leaves. The sun reflecting in the water droplets placed diamonds on its crown.

For many years in early spring, the white azalea budded even when there were only a few flowers. We remembered the person who knew: God is love.

Troy

He came running down the concourse at Kent County airport in Grand Rapids where our family was waiting for him. Experience had taught him to be polite; a beautiful smile flashed on his brown face, the face of a friendly salesman. Sadly, he was trying to sell himself.

His first hug was for me. Troy was thirteen and I was his sixth Mom. "Hi, Mom!" he said as if he was part of our family all his life.

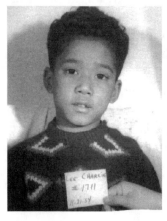

Troy

Looking at our group of seven "whites" and two Koreans, Troy, African-American, with mixed Korean parentage said, "Aunt Myrtle has told me everything about you."

Sophisticated, and worldly wise, he extended a hand to Claude, and then quickly turning to the kids, with the cunning of a teen, he followed the younger children to Peter's "souped up" green Chevy. I watched him shove next to Pete in the front seat, a boisterous kid who took Calvin's favorite spot.

The assistant director of the Holt adoption agency who escorted him told us on the way home, "Your son Peter may be a big help to that boy." He explained Troy's problems in his former families who could not cope with his insecurity that resulted in jealousy, dishonesty, stealing, and other ways of disturbing the good black families of which he had been a part.

We told him Aunt Myrtle had informed us of the bad experiences and the need for placing Troy in another family.

He was born to a fine woman in Korea, and his father was a prominent officer with the United States army. After several years, he left his young wife and her son for a new assignment elsewhere.

Troy spoke fluent English. He had attended the school for children of the American officers in Seoul, Korea. After a call to the Holt office, Troy's grandmother had brought the boy to a teahouse where she personally asked Mr. Harry Holt to find a well-to-do American family for him who would provide her grandson with a college education.

Impressed by the lady's sensitivity, Mr. Holt asked her, "Why do you want to release him?"

"In our culture, he is looked upon as less than a dog," she said with tears in her eyes. It is unusual for a Korean woman to show emotion. She often must try to smile while hurting inside.

For nine months, Troy was Mr. Holt's shadow at the orphanage at Ill-San, Korea. Then he went to a home where a grandmother ruled her extended family, and nobody gave Troy much attention.

Returning to the Holt ranch at Creswell, he went from there to Houston, Texas. There devoted parents thought their only child should have a brother, but Troy, competing for attention, made life unbearable for them. When they asked a social worker to take him to the Holt ranch again, the frustrated father lied, telling Troy they were taking a trip. Once at the airport, the man disappeared, leaving Troy in tears.

The social worker could give him some comfort, promising that he was going to be with his loving Grandpa Holt again at the ranch in Creswell. That hope was not realized. Harry Holt died unexpectedly of a heart attack in Korea. His concern for the suffering of orphans in the world broke the man's heart.

Troy found a family in New York who had adopted a girl. Having lost all faith in his parents, he found his way to the streets. After being severely beaten for skipping school, he ran away and slept on park benches until a police officer escorted him home.

His father, who worked for the American Airlines, placed him on a direct flight to Portland Oregon, phoning the Holt office to take him back.

For the time being, Auntie Myrtle gave Troy a home. It

was through her that we heard of him. At thirteen, he was a year younger than Judy and two years older than Ellie. With five children older and four younger, we hoped he might feel comfortable in our family.

Luckily when Troy arrived, it was the first week of summer vacation. I watched him as he ran up the trees like a cat in the back yard. He prowled around the house at night and in the daytime he inspected every corner of our house. One moment he was in the basement and Claude's shop, and the next up in our tree house painting old boards. I would holler, "Troy, change your clothes," but it was too late. He wanted to wear white jeans and a bright colored orange shirt and soon was covered with paint.

Hoping to distract him, I said, "The lawn needs mowing, Troy." He had paint from his hair to the soles of his shoes.

"I'll get the gas can. It'll wash this paint off too," he said.

Running behind him, I got the gas can in the nick of time. I filled the tank, and Troy was off with a whoop and a holler at top speed, criss-crossing the lawn, cutting around the picnic table chairs and over the hose and sprinklers, screaming at the kids who were excitingly trying to catch up with him.

"I won't charge you a dime for my service, Mom," he said. Pleased with himself, he told me, "Because you are the best Mom I ever had."

I hated to think what might happen the next day, but Claude always said, "One day at a time."

The kids in our street gathered the next morning in our back yard, and Troy got more attention than he needed. Playing hide and seek was a tame game after what happened the day before. As the group dispersed, I heard one shouting, "Here I come!" When finally I heard them say, "Home!" and thought everyone had been accounted for, the kids said, "Troy is not in, Mom. Have you seen Troy?"

"No, maybe he has gone to the bathroom."

Crash, crackle, kaplunk, a hell's racket as if the walls of our home collapsed! I rushed to the hallway hearing something shuffle in the bathroom. I opened the door, and in the bath tub behind the glass shower doors, a figure rose from the dust of plaster,

Troy! His black curly hair was covered by plaster and dust. Looking up at the ceiling, he said, "Mom?"

"Yes, I guess if you had to go through the ceiling, then this was the best place," I said.

I forgot to ask if he had been hurt, but he nimbly jumped from the tub, "I'll clean all of this up," he said with the look of a sick animal in his eyes.

Poor Troy, at least for a few hours it was quiet!

Claude heard the news when he parked the car in our driveway. "Dad! Dad! Troy fell through the ceiling!"

They pulled him to the downstairs bathroom, where he asked, "What? I don't see a hole."

"He fell in the bathtub, Dad."

"Oh, nobody will notice that unless someone takes a bath. There is no need to fix it immediately," Claude said. He was relieved that the bulkhead with shower doors were hiding the gaping hole.

At dinner time Troy began to talk again, bragging, "You wouldn't ever have found me if I hadn't slipped on that beam."

"Troy, we'll forget it. We will get used to it," Claude told him. "Learn to think before you do, son!"

We had no time for looking at the ceiling anyway. Everyone took a quick shower before the next one's turn!

On our first camping weekend, I learned Troy was a fanatic fisherman. He had brought his fishing pole along with the night crawlers that he picked on damp warm summer nights. Afraid that someone would steal his bait, he had hoarded the cans with dozens of fat crawlers under his bed. At breakfast time, he showed them off to the family, pulling one limp worm from the can after another. "Troy, you have to keep them cool, they'll die," I warned.

"O.K. Mom," he said. I found several cans hidden in the cool air register in his room.

I would scold him but he'd say, "I love ya' Mom. You're the best Mom I ever had!" I almost believed him.

Most of his clothes disappeared until only one pair of underwear and socks were left, but he didn't lose his orange colored shirts. We never found one stitch of the missing clothes. Our tablespoons were also lost, until an odor, a sour, mushy smell, led me to several partly empty soup and spaghetti cans in his clothes closet. Prowling through the house at night, he would have a snack and then hide the cans in his closet.

When changing his bed sheets, I found the torn seams. Strips of cotton laid in bunches with nylon hosiery under his bed. One Sunday morning Jane ran screaming from her bedroom wearing a pair of pantyhose with one leg cut off. "I'll kill him! I will, Mom! Troy's been in my drawers." I still was puzzled until the evidence was too strong for denial.

Troy, like all teenagers, was very conscious of his hair. It was slightly curly and shiny black so he tried to straighten it with globs of Vaseline. He then slipped a nylon stocking over his head and kept it in place with strips of his bed sheets which were slowly diminishing. Our neighbors must have questioned the origin of rags on my clothesline. They also were unhappy with a poodle Jane's friend had given her.

It was the stupidest and dirtiest animal of the breed. At dinnertime, she was a pest, so we tied her on a leash near the sliding doors since she had a habit of running away.

We expected a special sophisticated guest for dinner. I tried my very best to have a nice meal with interesting conversation. That in itself was difficult with the various members of our family in three different races around our table. All went well until the dessert and Troy shouted, "Hey, kids, look at Jackie. She is making puppies with Seeley's dog."

The six younger children ran to see what took place. The mating, in full view, was in progress and the conversation turned into a sex and fertility session. It would have been educational, except for the prudish woman who abhorred the show and lost her appetite for dessert.

Expectations rose as the weeks passed for Jackie to deliver. Yet Jackie, finally, totally ignorant of what happened to her, dropped four black puppies, one in the kitchen, a couple in the family room, and the last one on the living room carpet. Troy was elated when I picked them up and placed the new born with Jackie in a box near his bed. He claimed the largest gangly and ugliest pup for himself, naming her Julie.

"My Julie," he would say. The pup with soft curling hair matched his when the two lay on the floor, the dog cuddling near his head. They understood each other.

We had no trouble selling Jackie's three tightly curled puppies, and Jackie, too. I pitied her new owner if she had gold carpeting like ours! Too many times Jackie had chosen to relieve herself on the rug. Claude sanded the hardwood floor, and we gave it a new coat of varnish. But before it had time to dry, Troy had tracked over it. His footprints were still visible when we sold our home and moved to the Upper Peninsula of Michigan.

Julie and Troy trusted each other. She listened patiently to his problems, which he whispered in her ears. Unlike Troy, she knew who she was, not just a dog. She belonged to the world of people and needed to be loved, therefore giving generously of her love to all the family. But she really belonged to Troy!

Troy was fifteen and his fine family background showed he had inherited an easy going sophistication. He was intelligent, artistic and talented. He was also an insecure teenager, a charmer, a prince, but he did not produce in school. He did his homework, but lost it during the walk of four blocks to school. Girls liked him and knowing his temperament, we feared a confrontation.

When we adopted him legally, we told him he was our son

and that it was never going to change. For a middle name, he chose Peter. "I love my brother and my Mom and Dad too," he told the judge.

But Troy needed more discipline and a structured life that we could not give him. A friend of Peter's told us about Cal Farley's Boy's Ranch in Amarillo Texas. Troy and I wept in the back seat of the car on the way to Texas. "Mom, I love you and someday I'm going to be a Christian like you and Dad. And will you take good care of my Julie?" he asked.

"You are always our son," I said. "Remember we love you. When you graduate, we will come and Julie will never forget you!" We visited him several times, and on a trip to a board meeting in Oregon, I came unexpectedly. He was overjoyed. Spending the night alone in a motel, I cried myself to sleep, wishing we had had him as a small baby. He had told me, "Mom I love ya, but this has been happening too much to me."

He came home for Christmas, and two true friends were waiting for him, Jim who had stood by him in school and Julie, his dog. We all were happy to have him home, but on the last night he lied, saying he was at Jim's home. He had been with a girl, and we knew it was best for Troy to return to the Ranch. We were sadly relieved when the plane took him away and watched until we could not see it anymore through our tears. We missed him, doubting ourselves and his future.

"Some boys aren't ready to face the world after graduation from our program," the director at the Ranch told us. Troy wasn't, and we wished he could have been in an extended work situation. We later learned he was difficult, too difficult for further education at the Ranch. Our friends offered him work, and hoping to encourage him, we bought him a small Honda motorcycle. We thought he would learn responsibility by making payments. He swapped it for an old car and soon lost his job.

"Don't worry, Mom. I will pay you back. I love ya. You're the best Mom I ever had and someday I'll be a Christian," he would say. It was becoming more difficult to believe him now.

My position as a board member of the Holt Children's Service International, required a periodical assignment to Korea.

After returning from a two week absence, Claude told Troy to find a place of his own. Staying away at night and sleeping in the daytime, he took advantage of us. He stole money from his brothers and sisters and also shoplifted.

"Did you tell him that he always has a place in our family?" I asked my husband.

"Yes, he knows that. At twenty years old, he must learn responsibility."

He visited frequently. Then a week before Christmas he told me, "Mom, I've sold my car and I'm flying to New York to visit my former parents."

That afternoon he called again saying he was at the Greyhound station. Claude, taking time off from work, met him before the bus departed. With his stereo equipment and clothes packed in a box, he said good-bye, hugging Claude. He had a Bible in his hands and Claude said, "Troy, read the story of the son who left home. I will always be waiting for you and anxiously looking for your return."

Troy left a trail that was easy for us to follow. It went from New York, to Philadelphia, Houston and Los Angeles, from one former foster home to the next. We received an occasional letter and many bills from motels--the Ramada Inn, Holiday Inn and others. Troy had a good time using our name and address. He was of age and his expenses were not our responsibility.

We also received letters from girlfriends. I had returned several, except one written in beautiful calligraphy that I opened. A passionate sixteen year old girl wrote of her love for him and hoped she would be pregnant. "Now that you are home and in college and gone from me, I may have part of you in me, and always with me!" she wrote.

From her style of writing, I knew she had a loving home life. I returned her letter with a short note explaining Troy's problems. I assured her that we loved him too. She would never understand the reason and why. Neither did we ourselves.

Troy's phone call woke us up in the middle of the night. He was in San Antonio. "This is a tough world, Dad. I've been knifed. Someone tried to kill me. Will you ask Mom to send my papers? I am going to enlist in the Navy in San Diego." He didn't, but he did ask to be stationed at Great Lakes, Illinois.

Three months after that call, he came home in uniform having completed basic training.

Returning home from my bus route, I found our excited children shouting, "Mom, Troy is home. He has a hat full of money and said he would be back for a good home cooked dinner."

"You'll be rich, Mom. He'll pay you back the money he owes you for the Honda!"

"Troy? With a hat full of money? We don't see him back!" Claude said.

His brothers and sisters left the best pieces of chicken on the platter for our son who did not return to us. He didn't return to his base either. He went A.W.O.L., was arrested and spent some time in the Kent County jail. Six months and one week later, the navy discharged him.

He visited us again with a cute girl and she told him, "Didn't I tell you, Troy? Go home more often."

She was very mature and well-mannered. Before they left, I once more heard him say, "I'll pay you back Mom; and I'll be a Christian like you, but not yet. I want to have fun. Life looks like so much fun to me!"

"Troy, do you really have fun?" I asked.

"Not yet, but it will be, Mom!"

The girl wisely left us alone and it gave me a chance to tell him, "Troy, don't you dare hurt this girl and make her pregnant!"

"Oh, Mom, you know I..."

"No, Troy you have to prove that now!" I said.

Ellie met him once more working in the hospital. He hadn't been home for a long time. "Troy, go home and see Mom and

Dad," she said.

"I can't. Too much is happening to me," he told her.

He lived with so-called friends, taking advantage of them until they tired of his freeloading and running up phone bills and threw him out. The police regularly came to our door investigating shoplifting and minor complaints. He had been stealing steaks from a freezer stored in a garage. We knew he lived in Grand Rapids, moving so often we could not keep in touch.

On Labor Day weekend of 1977, Claude and I were taking a three day vacation at our new home, Peter built this home for us in the Upper Peninsula of Michigan near Little Girl's Point and five miles from Lake Superior. Since we had made a trip to Korea and adopted John Kim, a thirteen year old boy who had polio at a

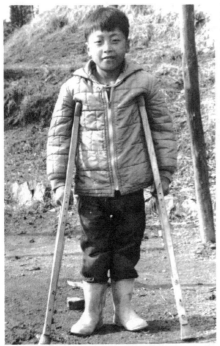

young age, the two of us had not had time off without our children. John was a spunky kid and had been raised in a reliable, safe environment of the Holt orphanage. He learned quickly, was independent, and sure of himself. His goal of a college education was nearly impossible for a crippled orphan in Korea.

The five teenage children were staying at the home of our married children in Grand Rapids for the few days we were gone. It was a beautiful week-end. Claude

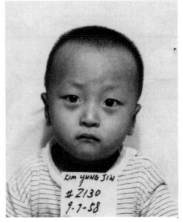

John

189

finished some small projects on our home, and I enjoyed hiking in the forest. On Sunday evening we drove to Lake Superior. Taking a stroll along the shore, we watched the sunset. The Lake was smooth like a mirror when we climbed the high cliff and viewed the gray silhouettes of the Porcupine Mountains. I knew there were many miles to the northern shores of Lake Superior and to Canada and everything was so peaceful. I sat down on a large log and imagined the broad rays of a fast sinking sun on the lake were a golden path to heaven.

Praying for each of our children as if they were near me, I began to mention Kathy first, then Anne and Jane, Peter, Judy. Coming to Troy, I worried, much more than usual, and prayed to keep him with Ellie, Amy, John, Calvin and Alvin, all in God's care.

Claude returned with an interesting piece of driftwood. "Well, it is time to go home now," he said. I reluctantly left. It was so peaceful, and the following morning we had to go downstate again.

Turning in the driveway, we noticed the bright warning lights of a state police cruiser following. Stopping behind us, the officer asked Claude, "Are you Mr. Van Ooyen?"

"Yes."

"Do you have a son, Troy?"

"Yes."

"Well, sir. There was a homicide this morning in Grand Rapids."

"Is Troy dead?" I asked.

"Yes, Ma'am. You may call the State police at the Wyoming post in Lower Michigan."

We were numb. Troy? We had worried about our aged parents, but our mischievous Troy, dead?

I heard him saying, "Mom, you are the best. Someday I'll be a Christian like you and Dad, but not yet. This looks too much like fun."

We drove to the Omans at the agate shop near Little Girl's Point and asked if we could use their phone. The detective at the state police post told us that Troy had been stabbed thirteen times by the jealous boyfriend of a girl he was seeing. "If it is any comfort to you, he died instantly."

I could not weep. There were no tears but a heaviness in my chest and throat that was impossible to swallow.

Again the old anger and hate made me sick and then there was also the big question, "Amy, can't you trust me?"

"Lord, why?" I asked. "Please help me to trust you."

We had hundreds of questions as we drove the long miles home. Claude raised a practical question, "Where do we get the money for a burial? We've two homes, no savings right now."

I heard myself say, "We must trust God for that." But I really was thinking, "This is not true. I can't believe what I said."

It was very real for our children at home. "Mom and Dad, don't look at TV and the newspaper. It's the big news and has been repeated several times," Anne said.

Early on Tuesday morning, the secretary where Troy worked called. "Mrs. Van Ooyen, my sympathy. Through our insurance agent, Mr. Jahgar, I heard of your musical family. His son also plays in the Grand Rapids Youth Symphony. Last Friday, Troy was in my office and he signed up for a life insurance benefit of four thousand dollars. Your name is the beneficiary. Maybe the papers are in his car that was impounded by the state police."

When I went to the state police office to get Troy's car, the detective understandingly gave me his condolences saying, "Mrs. Van Ooyen, I will tell you I have read over Troy's records of minor offenses. He was at the wrong place and died, defending a young woman whose boyfriend came to kill her. Troy jumped him and received what was intended for his girlfriend."

He reflected awhile and then said, "Mrs. Van Ooyen, right now a young woman with a child is waiting in the foyer. Please don't speak to her. Please forgive me, but that girl was not worth dying for." Visibly disturbed, he took off his glasses and led me to the door.

I passed the girl and did not take a good look at her. Knowing what a fine man this officer was gave me some comfort. I needed to search Troy's car. He had done a good paint job on it and a bumper sticker read, "Get high on marijuana." Inside was the smell of "Brut," his favorite cologne. He seemed so close. The insurance papers lay under the back seat with a receipt for the stereo equipment. I found three class rings from high school girls in the glove compartment and a driver's license renewal.

Our friend, who is a funeral director assisted us, suggesting we buy an economical burial site out of town. I then bought a bright orange shirt and a pair of jeans for our Troy.

He looked so much older without his beautiful smile and mischievous dark sparkling eyes closed. It was not him with his nimble hands still.

I could not weep for him, not with tears. The four thousand dollar check cried out, "Some day Mom, I'll pay you back!"

We anguished about the three thousand dollars left in our bank account. We wanted to spend it, but for what?

Peter, who by now was teaching in Vancouver B.C. Canada, called, "Dad, is Mom home? Who will be coming to our wedding?"

We had almost forgotten that Peter and Colleen were going to be married in October.

"Peter, Dad and I will come and those who can afford it. I am not sure who all will make it to your wedding," I said.

"I wish that the whole family could come, but that would cost too much and is probably impossible," he said.

Hearing the longing and a hint of disappointment in his voice, gave me an idea. "I guess we'll have to wait and see what happens," I said, keeping my thoughts of using Troy's money a secret until Claude agreed.

With the three thousand dollars, we bought airline tickets for all his brothers and sisters, who were still in school and college, to attend Peter and Colleen's wedding as a memorial to Troy.

On the evening of his wedding day, we surprised him. Waiting for our arrival, Peter counted us walking through the line at customs. "They are all here, everyone. All the family is here!" He shouted at Colleen who stood beside him.

We celebrated for two days, Colleen's family provided the transportation. On Sunday morning, we all went to church and later in the afternoon toured the beautiful city in a rented school bus.

Auntie Myrtle joined us too, driving up from California.

We arrived home in the evening on Monday, with the lasting memory of the eventful trip. For a short time, the balance in our savings account was erased until I received another call from Troy's work place. The secretary told me, "Mrs. Van Ooyen, Troy's death has been declared an accident. The insurance company will send you a check for four thousand dollars because you deserve a double indemnity in his case."

Was Troy flashing his beautiful smile? Claude believed he would have!

I could only leave that to God. The very heavy obstruction in my throat still shut off all tears.

Tears for Troy

Rush! Rush! It is Sunday morning. Everyone runs and hurries to be ready for church.

"I'm going," Dad says, hoping to escape the confusion by starting the old model station wagon.

"Dad is waiting," one of the boys warns, the girls still fussing with their hair and makeup.

One by one, we stumble out of the door, and, with a sigh, I seat myself in the front next to my husband.

"My hair, please close the windows," one of the girls begs.

It is always an unholy ten minutes before we drive down the hill on the way to church. I look back at the five teenagers. All seems well, but there is a nagging feeling something is different this morning. "Did I forget to turn on the oven for the Sunday roast?"

Alvin asks, "Dad, what is that lying on the road?"

"It's something black. Is it our Julie?" Eleanor is right.

"Julie, who has seen our Julie? Now I know we did not see her this morning. That's what was missing. It must be Julie."

My husband drives on, passing the black form on the road. There's not much left but hair, soft curly black hair. Yes, it is our dog, Troy's dog, until she became my dog. Actually, Julie belonged to our family. She was one of us.

Only on Sunday mornings was she a dog, segregated from her people who go to church. She knew, and would slip away from all the commotion and go down to the basement, her tail drooping. Sometimes she'd look at me questioning, but often not, with her head down she would slink quietly down the basement stairs, dejected. I could feel her disappointment for being different.

Some of the children glance back at the black spot on the asphalt, but nobody says anything and all look worried at me. My husband keeps on driving and in silence we arrive at the parking lot of our church.

"We'll have to bury her," I say as we enter thechurch.

The organist is playing a loud and joyous prelude as we solemnly file in the pew. The music is clashing with my feelings. I sit straight and stiff, bracing the flood of noise. This is not right! I hate all this loud triumphant sound.

When the congregation is singing the first hymn, it makes me angry, very angry! This is all wrong. I don't want to sing. I see that black curly hair and a mangled form on the road. The hair matched Troy's hair, our adopted son, who was killed.

It was his dog. He named her Julie, and then she became my dog. How can the people sing and sing? Julie is dead, and Troy is dead, and I am alone with all these people. One tear trickles slowly down my cheek, then another, one more. Amy looks sideways; her big brown eyes are worried.

Ellie gives me a tissue. "Mom, people are looking at you," she whispers.

I keep staring straight ahead. So what? Do I care? I'm angry, mad, very mad.

"Mom, you can't cry in church!" Ellie puts her hand on my arm.

Drip! Drip! Drip! Cry? I'm not crying. Just, drip...drip, one tear at a time as I think about our Julie. She was so faithful, and I remember how she once came to me when I was fishing. She swam across Moosehead Lake, then Little Presque Isle Lake too, and found me in a sheltered cove. She was dead tired when I lifted her into the boat, too tired to shake herself dry in the stern. She slept contentedly for an hour. She was a good fishing companion, always happy for what I caught, no matter how little, and she never was in the way for a good cast. A log drifting in the lake became her enemy, and a rock washed by the waves was something to growl at.

She was smart, but no show-off, never in command, always following. She understood more than we wanted her to know.

How could this have happened? She was not a roamer. She would never go into the road.

We had been planning to leave for a vacation early the next morning, a camping trip to the U.P.of Michigan. Peter had cut the boy's hair yesterday and also trimmed Julie. She loved all that attention.

I remembered how much Troy loved her and how he had trained her. We all loved Julie.

What? Were we to sing again? Another hymn, how inappropriate, and everyone is standing now. I do too, glaring at the people, and keep dripping one tear at a time.

We sit down again and I decide no one will touch what is left of Julie. I will scrape what is left of her off the road and bury her. And no one is going to help me or see me do that. This is my job!

The sermon drones on. Eleanor gives me another tissue. Amy looks more worried. My husband pretends to listen to the preacher and the boys are restless. I don't care. Drip...drip...drip! Will this service ever end?

When it is finally over, I've buried Julie mentally and am prepared to face reality.

Looking neither left nor right, ignoring friendly church people, I walk straight to the car.

"Mom, everyone was looking at you," Amy says.

"So what? Who would understand?"

Ellie asks, "Are you mad, Mom?"

"Yes, I am! I'm stinking mad. I'm angry, and I'm going to bury Julie!"

"Oh, no, we'll do it. Don't Mom," Alvin says.

"Amy, that is not your job, I will," my husband says.

"Well, Mom, don't worry too much. She's had a good life and she was ugly. She's had a haircut and a nice meal before she died. When I came home last night there was a dead pheasant on the road and she probably ate it." Calvin, always practical had the answer. So, that's how she was killed.

"You all keep quiet. I can't stand you all talking about her," I said.

"Quiet!" my husband told the children. "Mom will be all right."

"Oh, I'm glad he understands," I thought.

Coming up on the hill, we all look for Julie. There is no Julie; she's gone.

Once at home, the good aroma of a roast in the oven smells like Sunday morning. I am sad now, a heavy sadness lingering came after a cup of coffee with a slice of cake. The children notice my changing mood and all at once everyone is talking, praising Julie. "She was a good dog," John says, "the best dog we ever had."

"She was ugly though, but nice. She met me at the door last night and might have slipped out," Calvin admits.

A knock on the door and the neighbor living down the hill enters. "You lost your dog last night," he says.

Then he explains that early this morning he went to mass and found Julie lying on the road. "My wife told me, 'the Van Ooyens love that dog. This is horrible.' So we came home before you did and decided it was better we bury her. I put her in a nice box and she's resting under that big pine tree in front near the road. If you like, you may put a marker there."

As my husband thanked the kind neighbor, the five teenagers eager to console me and maybe hoping to find comfort themselves, left. They said, "We will be looking in the field for a perfect headstone for Julie's grave."

Tears began to flow, a stream of tears, not one at a time, drip...drip...drip!

It was finally quiet. My husband asked, "Are you still angry, Amy?"

"No, I was not angry at you; I was angry at God. I loved that kid," I said."

Camping

*T*he raindrops pounding a steady rhythm on the tent roof made me snuggle a little deeper into the sleeping bag. Trying to avoid a bump underneath the inflated air mattress, I heard the leaves of the poplar trees near shore gossip. Like a bunch of old women shaking their heady branches, they whispered, "You are crazy!"

Louder now, encouraged by a gust of wind across the lake, they said, "Crazy, yes, stupid and crazy!"

One of our children groaned, stirring in his sleep. Another was grinding his teeth. And in the distance, a great owl asked, "Who? Whoo's there?"

"We!" On the hill at Moosehead Lake in the U.P., too excited to find sleep, we were slowly recuperating from an annual bout with "Tent-itis."

Our first trip to the Upper Peninsula of Michigan nine years before gave us the camping bug. Since then, we have tried to cure it with a dose of Down-State picnicking. When the younger child-

Hauling in Fish

ren were too small for rugged outdoor living, we rented a small cottage that was very reasonable! We had so many mouths to feed, we tried to stretch our vacation budget with pork and beans, macaroni and cheese, and pancakes, supplemented by the little blue gills I caught.

For ten years Bitely Lake and Goudswards cottage was our Eldorado where we were exploring the woods and lakes. But two weeks are only a temporary remedy for the deep forest and the shores of Lake Superior in the wild North country of the U.P.

"Who, whooo is here?"

Even the waves announced our presence, applauding loudly against the granite rocks on shore.

"They're here again!" a loon answered.

Its yodeling woke one of the girls. "Mom, what's that noise?" she asked.

"Shuss, a loon!" I listened to the ancient cry heard since the beginning of time; my life was touching God and creation.

At dawn, long before the sun peeked across the scrawny balsam trees on shore, the fishing fever took hold. Julie, our cockerpoo, happily waved her tail, greeting me.

"Be quiet," I told her. "It is only for the two of us. We go fishing."

She ran to the boat and sat in position on the stern, and we were kindred souls! Growling at a dead log drifting in the lake, she was jealous of anything robbing the peaceful hour.

Later, when Claude's splashing paddle splattered my trance, revealing a bright new day, the real world returned.

"I brought you a cup of coffee," he said.

On the end of his four by eight foot paddle board, the coffee perked balancing on a small camp stove.

"Claude, this is incredible. One wobble, and the kaboodle slides to the bottom of the lake!"

He laughed. "I brought you a few cookies too."

Nimble, stable and poised, he poured my coffee.

It has not ever tasted so good. I watched him returning to camp, knowing it was time to quit. My family was waiting and hungry for breakfast.

Claude and His Paddle Board

"Mom, you didn't keep all the little ones!"

The three boys who welcomed me were suspicious, knowing too well that it was their job to fillet the fish.

"U.P. fish aren't small, and these have lots of good meat," I said.

"Leave some with the tails on. Those are my favorite and crunchy, like fried bacon," Amy said. She hurried back to throw more wood on the campfire. It didn't take long and breakfast was ready.

Our frying pan, thirty inches in diameter at the bottom, held ten pancakes at a time and was the envy of nearby campers. A retired couple observing us and tempted by the activity stopped by asking, "Do you know what day it is?"

"I believe it is Wednesday," I said.

"John, our daughter's birthday was yesterday. We were supposed to be at Ontonogan." She was shocked.

"Can't keep track of time in this country." The man was reluctant to break up camp. "You have a healthy bunch of kids. We've enjoyed watching them," he said.

"Of course, John. Them pancakes got hymns fried right in, she was singing!" his wife said, pulling her husband to camp.

I was sorry for the couple who were to leave for a late birthday party.

Had I really been singing? If so, then on this beautiful day, all of nature rejoiced.

The old garbage can which we used for a fish creel had been tied to the end of a log on shore and was raided, not that the boys were sorry. Calvin and John filleting the fish, with Alvin "skinning," detested the job that created a fierce competition. They had told me the second side of the fish is always much more difficult to slice, and all were experts who criticized each other.

The Catch

"John, you leave too much meat on the bone!"

"No, I don't. Look, I can see through the skeleton right at your ugly face, Cal."

"I see your face through this piece of meat." Alvin peered in his fillet. "Poor work, John."

"You left too much meat on the skin!" Smack! Taking revenge, John threw half a fish at Al who ducked for shelter under the picnic table.

The fish were a mixed blessing, and Mom sometimes, accompanied by one of the girls, kept on catching more fish! Now the bounty was disappearing, could it be? No, they wouldn't! Maybe it was a camper, someone who envied our fish meals and was tempted!

We fried fish fillets for breakfast, fish patties at lunch time, and a fish snack at night. Wasn't the aroma at our camp the talk of everyone?

Now not needing an excuse for my fishing fever, I kept the little fish too and the boys protested loudly until Claude found the solution.

"No, Dad! Please, Dad, oh yuck!"

The shouting at camp aroused my curiosity, and I rowed to shore where five kids were either wailing or begging Claude, who demonstrated his invention and seemed determined to prove to them a valuable point.

Puzzled by his turning a contraption fastened to the roof of our old station wagon, I wondered what he was doing now.

"Dad, this is awful. I can't stand this. Mom, make Dad quit!" Ellie came running for me to the boat.

I heard Claude say, "Put another fish in, one more!"

"What is going on?"

"We are going to eat fish balls," Claude said. "That fighting about fish cleaning has been enough to drive me crazy, and since you keep those dinky little fish, I'll grind them all up, bones, tails, and everything. You won't even have to gut them."

He was steadily cranking the handle of an old fashioned meat grinder he had bought at a garage sale. A grayish watery gook dropped in a pan held by Alvin who was nearly in tears.

"Dad, we'll never argue again if we don't have to eat this," Calvin said.

"I'm sure Mom knows a recipe for tasty fish balls. There are a few fish left. Get them in there now."

Feeling contrite about the small fish, I asked, "Bones and all?"

"Sure, it is calcium in our diet. We need it!"

My mind raced, a recipe, he had said. Often substituting and cooking with what was available had not been difficult, but this would be a challenge.

That evening a sour faced sad group peeked at the menu on the table as Claude said thanks for the meal.

The smell was not bad. I had decided to mix the awful stuff with Bisquick, adding eggs, salt and spices, much like Swedish meatballs, but smaller. For consolation, I had fried hush puppies.

"Us Southerns always fry those alongside our catfish," an elderly camper escaping the heat in Alabama had said when she gave me her recipe.

Claude tasted the first fish ball, chewing it bravely down. He passed the rest on and said,"Not bad. This will save you boys a lot of work. Aren't you hungry?"

I took a little one and watched Ellie sneaking hers under the table to Julie. The dog took it, licked on it and sneezed. The boys were pretending to choke theirs down.

"We've all learned our lesson Claude," I said and placed a

larger bowl with "Huussh Poppies" on the table, trying to imitate a southern accent, it produced a wry smile of relief from the kids.

"We're sorry, Dad." Calvin spoke for the rest of us!

We haven't had a need for fish balls since because I did not keep the little ones, and if I had, the boys would not have dared to complain.

On my last evening of fishing, the sun cast a rosy glow on a dead white birch. I noticed a young doe with her fawn come to take a drink. She hesitated, watch-ing me closely, her coat a rich orange brown. She was nursing her little one. Cautiously maneuvering my boat so as not to disturb them, I rowed along shore.

Around a small bay, I spot-ted our log with the fish creel and surprised the thief right in his act. Selecting a nice crappie, the blue heron swallowed it whole, dipping in for more, taking my prize bass. He was probably sure I would catch more the next day. Unfortunately for him and all of us, we were to leave for home.

We stared at the flames of our last campfire; each one having good memories of people telling their own stories. Some tales were without words, others expressed themselves in a song. Always in the background there were the voices of children, shouting or hol-lering for a chance at kick the can, playing a game by moonlight.

We had many campfires down-state in our back yard, at Bitely cottage, or on the fourth of July and Labor Day at Shelby Beach on the sand dunes near Lake Michigan.

The suspense of the wild connecting us with those who were here long before us, and shuffling noises of creatures lurking behind our backs in the dark forest of the U.P. don't tell us their secrets. They make us huddle closer to each other and the fire.

When all were sleeping, I once more walked to the shore of the lake listening to the night.

The chatting poplars never cease to be quiet. Trying to keep it a secret, they whispered about me, not knowing I understood their language. "She'll return and someday thrust her roots deep in our soil," they said.

Packed for Vacation

Eel Lake Cabin

"Someday we will buy land," Claude promised, "a small parcel that will be ours."

We were crossing the long bridge that spans the Straits of Mackinaw toward Michigan's lower peninsula, returning home from a month-long camping vacation in the U.P., and I had wiped away a tear. "Air pollution," I told the children. "Late August is hay fever time."

The children were eagerly looking forward to seeing their friends again, tired of travel and camping in remote forest campgrounds. "I'm lonesome for Cindy," Alvin said. Cindy was the neighbor's dog.

I never grew lonesome for anything downstate. I wiped another tear, blew my nose, and reflected on Claude's idle promise. Buy land in the U.P.? Impossible. A crazy idea of my husband, the impractical optimist. I knew he was hoping to console me. He didn't buy that hay fever thing.

Buy land? Where would we get the money? We had eleven children; seven in college and high school, four in grade school. That made for a tight budget! Claude worked many hours overtime to support the family, which cost more and more every year.

I looked sideways at his serious face, smiled through my tears and squeezed his hand. "Sure," I said. We'll buy land. Some day." But I didn't believe it.

For fifteen years we had vacationed in the U.P. Its forests, lakes, waterfalls, and Lake Superior's rocky shores and sandy beaches were part of our lives.

"Why must we always go up north?" the children would ask, but Claude and I would never hear them. We loved the U.P. vacations and built trips around a variety of interests. One year we focused on waterfalls, another year on traveling the shore of Lake

Superior. One summer we explored the history of mining. And of course, we always looked for the best fishing spots or canoe routes where we might discover wildlife. For Claude and me, Michigan's Upper Peninsula was everything.

Then one day it happened, and we found ourselvess driving 500 miles north from our home near Grand Rapids to a secluded part of the Ottawa National Forest near Marenisco. Friends from the U.P. had phoned. A lake cabin in the National Forest was for sale. They warned us that the cabin needed repair, but knowing our love for the area, felt we might be interested. "We think the owner will sell if we come along as references," they said.

It was early May. In the U.P. spring comes late, so we drove cautiously, watching for deer that feed on spring grass sprouting between patches of snow. As we neared Watersmeet, a deer suddenly bounded in our path, bounced off the bumper, and disappeared in the forest. The car continued to purr, but then we heard a loud hiss. We limped into the only gas station and motel for miles around and took a room to await morning.

While trying to rest, I thought about our dream of a cabin in the forest near a lake. It had seemed an impossible dream, but we had nurtured it for years and shared it with friends. Now it seemed the dream could become reality.

In the morning, the gas station repairman examined our car and found the radiator had been punctured by the fan due to the impact of the deer. "I'll get a neighbor to drive you to your friends at Langford Lake," he said. "Don't worry. Your car will be ready this afternoon."

At Langford Lake we met our friends and drove in their car to Eel Lake at the end of a winding, narrow road in the Ottawa National Forest. There we found the cottage of our dreams, we, a man and woman from Holland.

The owner had not arrived, and we looked out over the lake, musing. "How did I get to this place in the wilderness of the U.P. ?" I asked myself. A pair of loons drifted lazily in the sunlight. What made us leave the safety of dikes that kept back the North Sea and move to the United States of America?

Why did we leave the confinement of an overpopulated

country? Could it have been the same hunger for freedom to roam and explore that now made me want to buy an old cedar log cabin?

I walked out on the old crumbling dock. A small yellow perch lay parallel to the dock like a miniature torpedo, its fins pumping the rhythm of fish life. "Grow up, little fish," I said. "We'll be neighbors next summer, just wait and see!" Bulrushes and cattails growing sparsely along the shore rustled their approval.

Claude joined me on the dock. "What did you say?" he asked.

"Claude, I want this little cabin, and I just told the fish so."

"I want it too," Claude said.

"Is it bad to want something so very much?" I asked.

"It depends. We'll wait until the owner comes. What's her name?"

"Mary, Mary Young. She is selling the cabin because the Forest Service ordered her to make expensive repairs. Is it possible that we could buy it?"

I hoped Claude would say yes, although I knew he seldom gave a direct yes or no. Always I get a cautious, indirect answer.

"The walls are sturdy," he said.

I looked up toward the cabin built of vertical cedar logs, so black and mildewed by many harsh U.P. winters. I didn't know why I wanted the small cabin so desperately, but I did. With all my heart I desired those white birch reaching for sunlight and the soft green balsams and cedars. I wanted the glittering lake and that little fish when it grew up. I wanted all of it!

Suddenly cheap blaring music shattered the quiet. From behind the trees a little old lady approached. She wore a bright red pant suit and carried a pocket radio. Chattering above the music, she explained that she had come along the lake shore to avoid the hill behind the cabin.

"Where is my Loon?" she asked. "Have you seen my papa Loon? Where are you? Hoo hoo! she yodeled. A western pop tune from a radio strapped to her wrist clashed with all the nature around us. She did not introduce herself, but we knew she must be Mary Young, owner of the cabin.

Constantly jabbering, Mary showed us a huge ring with dozens of keys. "I had some extras made for you folks," she said. "Three of each. This one is for the front door, this one for the back. That little one is for the boat, and this one must be for the outhouse. We have a key for the gasoline can too. My husband built this cabin, but he is gone. We don't understand why, but he died on Christmas Day, didn't he Gladys?"

Only then did we notice Gladys. She was thin and seemed to be wasting away from some disease. Dressed in black, she was almost invisible, a small shadow following Mary.

"I'm Gladys," she said, snatching a puff from her cigarette. She gave us a sad smile and coughed.

"Gladys is my sister-in-law," Mary said. She chattered on cheerfully. "Her husband died too, so we live in my house. Do you like my cabin? Deany, my husband was not well when he tried to repair the roof."

Suddenly she looked helpless. "The Forest Service keeps reminding me that I must fix this place, and because I can't, I have

to sell it. My Deany was so happy here. He built it in 1950."

She talked and talked, repeating herself while we waited. The keys rattled and Mary's twittering disturbed the peace, but not the cabin! Its cedar logs formed a stronghold against Mary's onslaughts. She tried to find the key for the door. Claude asked kindly if he could help but received only a vague answer. "This must be the right key. No, that one. No?" Reluctantly, she let Claude try, and he soon opened the door.

Mary entered first. Pointing proudly to the door, she said, "See the claw marks? Bear. You must be careful here, you know. Bears come at dusk, so keep the door locked."

The fresh forest air gave way to the musty smell of wet, molding clothes, mothballs, and mouse urine. No! I thought, this horrible stinking place is not fit for living.

Holes the size of a man's fist near the chimney opened up to the sky. Firewood in the old wood box sprouted mushrooms. It was evident that rain and snow had kept this cabin damp for years. Mary found a handful of sawdust behind a day bed. "You naughty carpenter ants are back," she said. "Gladys, do we have any Raid here?"

The other woman had not followed us inside, but I heard her cough and utter a strangled no.

The ceiling of imitation wood-grain cardboard exposed three squirrel nests with strips of cedar and cotton protruding from gaping holes. No, this dank dungeon is not for us, I thought.

Feeling nauseated, I fled to the lake, wondering if the view from the dock had been a mirage. The wail of a loon echoed across the silver water as the bird raised high, stretching his wings to claim the lake for himself and his mate. The perch was still there. "I'm crazy, but I want this place," I said stubbornly. Some cottage!

As I stood on the dock, I could hear Mary Young talking a torrent, a never-ending stream of words. Claude's deep voice stated with quiet persistence his evaluating of costs and materials needed for repairs.

Looking at the dilapidated building and remembering the stench, I smiled. " A summer home?" Then noticing Gladys who had folded her body like a sick bird at the rotting picnic table, I joined her. She smiled, coughed and waited quiet and dignified. Steps muffled by humus and pine needles made me look up. It was Claude. He came to give me his verdict.

We walked toward the dock. "Do you still like this place, Amy?"

"Will it forever smell like that?" I asked, needing encouragement. My dream was fading fast !

"The building is solid," Claude said. "It sits on a firm foundation. The floor is not bad, except near the chimney where it is rotting. The roof will need work, but it looks worse than it really is. I can fix the building, but you will have to do the rest."

'Will we tell Mary we'll buy her cabin?" I asked.

"Not unless she'll stop talking! he answered. Then he said thoughtfully, "Can we afford it? She is asking $1200."

"No," I said. "We can't. But we'll manage. All our children will pitch in and enjoy this place. We'll move in with the mice and squirrels and with the porcupine that lives under the floor of the

outhouse and the bats that raise a family between the posts and paneling on the east wall."

"Well, you'll never be lonesome here," Claude teased. "Loving wild creatures like you do."

I nodded. "Let's buy it."

*Frisian Flag
at Eel Lake*

Cairn

Claude exchanged a down payment check with Mary Young for all her keys. Sensing her loss, for a moment she stopped talking. Then she began again to tell us of her husband Deany who had built the cabin and how he had loved this place so much. Understanding that her dream would never end and that it would always be Deany's cabin, Claude gave her the extra key to the front door and invited her to come often for a visit.

We watched the little old lady in the red pant suit disappear among the green balsam, Gladys following, still quiet and barely visible. We heard the radio fading, and in the distance a loon laughed, freeing us of our guilt for having bought someone else's dream with cash.

Our Home in the Woods

"We think Mom has spring fever!" the children told Claude one evening early in March.

"You mean she's ready to go fishing?" he asked. My rod and reel were waiting for me in the corner of our bedroom.

Yes, spring had arrived, and as usual it had the children worried for they knew that spring meant the annual spring cleaning rite. Hoping their father might think of some way to escape the danger, they looked to him for help. Counting Dad with the kids, it was eight to one, but they all knew I would win in the end and everyone would be drafted to do their part in cleaning the house from attic to cellar. Walls were to be washed, floors waxed, and worst of all, closets organized until Mom's spring fever had run it's course. Then she could go fishing.

Sometimes, when I was lucky, March gave us one of those wonderful sticky snowstorms which canceled schools for a day. I made good use of these snow days! We found lost scissors and pens, unreturned library books, and jewelry that the girls had accused each other of losing. Even a dollar bill was retrieved from its hiding place. But best of all, socks separated for months found a patiently waiting mate and were reunited. In the end all were happy, knowing it would be another year before Mom would have another attack of spring fever as my daughter Amy called it.

But those hectic days were soon forgotten as we anticipated spring vacation and a trip to our Eel Lake cabin in the U.P. Not wanting to waste any time, we left after school was out one Friday afternoon in late March. We drove across the Mackinaw bridge at night, admiring the mighty structure illuminated against the dark sky.

Leaving early in the morning for the western part of the U.P., we reached the National Forest road that led to our cabin by late afternoon. A snowstorm the day before had transformed the woods into a fairyland, perfect for skiing to the cabin waiting for us five miles down the road.

Reluctant to be first to desecrate the white sculptured beauty, we decided to take turns, but the children pushed ahead of Claude and me. Taking a short cut across Eel Lake, they found the hidden key and started a fire in the cabin.

In no hurry, we followed the longer forest trail to the steps that led over the hill. Climbing slowly we carried our skis and sank deep when we missed a step hidden by the snow.

From the top of the hill, the scene was exactly as we dreamed it would be during the long winter. The small cottage lay hidden under the evergreens, mostly balsams, their snow-laden branches folded like an umbrella, patiently waiting for spring to relieve their burden.

With all my heart I again said Yes to this place. If only we could live here permanently!

The days of that early vacation were filled with cross country skiing, exploring the nearby lakes, reading, and playing games. Dean Young's old sports magazines dating from 1950 and Mary's old magazines with old-fashioned hair styles and clothes gave our teenage girls bursts of hysterical laughter.

Having to melt snow for cooking water, our coffee tasted somewhat herbal. Perhaps fine evergreen needles added the unexpected flavor. Clean snow mixed with coolaid and sugar made delicious snow cones for the kids. Birds and animals came for a hand out, appreciating our leftover scraps.

A week later, skiing back to our car, we seemed almost to have lost track of days. On the windshield, a slip of paper told us that we had been recognized by the friendly folks in nearby Marenisco. "Welcome, don't get lost!" the note said. Another note added, "See you in spring!"

Savoring the warmth of being welcome, we left the forest behind and drove to Ironwood for the second reason of our vacation trip. Friends had informed us that forty acres of wooded land were for sale North of Ironwood. The property was located near Lake Superior, five miles from Little Girl's Point. Following the realtors directions, we came to a two-track road that led to a hunting camp built on the forty-acre parcel.

The children, skeptical but adventurous, stared at the old building covered with imitation asphalt siding, its door swinging sadly in the wind.

"Oh no! Is this where we are going to live?" one asked. "It's worse than Eel Lake cabin!"

"Will we be poor when Dad retires?" Ellie said, looking at me with a worried expression.

"I don't like this place!" echoed Amy after her sister.

Claude calmly quieted the group. "We're just looking, not buying. Not yet, anyway."

I was not so sure. I knew he liked these private woods a half-mile from the main road and ten miles from town. Questioning my own courage for a lifestyle so far from neighbors, I had my doubts.

"Here's an outhouse, but some animal ate part of it!" Alvin shouted.

"Oh, porcupines; they'll eat anything. They like salt," Calvin informed us. "I read about it, Dad. Even the tires of your car aren't safe." It was plain he hoped to discourage Claude from buying this place. My husband did not answer Calvin.

"The price is much too high," Claude said thoughtfully inspecting the cabin. "It's not very well built." He looked at me, expecting an answer.

"Where will we go to school? What is there to do?" the children asked over and over.

Remembering our adequate home in Grandville, I said, "Don't worry!" But I lied to myself. I was worrying.

Returning to town, we left the children at McDonalds, assuring the hungry teenagers that hamburgers and French fries were still available a short drive from the woods. Then Claude and I went to the realtor and made an offer, just half of what he had asked for the property.

The children felt quite secure, believing we would never move them to those Upper Peninsula woods. While Claude wished the offer would be accepted, I was caught, as often had happened before, somewhere in between.

But during our first week back home, a telephone call settled the matter. The realtor told us the owner had "reluctantly" accepted our offer and he would close the deal upon the arrival of our check. So that was how we became owners of forty acres and another old cabin, this one near Lake Superior.

Our four married children were even less enthusiastic about the new property than were the younger ones. They reminded us we were getting older. "Your friends move to condominiums to retire," they said. "They all go to a warmer climate. You will freeze up there! And it's too far away! We will miss you too much."

Their arguments could not persuade us to change our decision. We were not going to retire just yet. In the years to come, our five younger children needed an education like the older ones had enjoyed.

Our eldest son Peter was more optimistic. "Our parents are different," he told the girls. "They are naturalists, and a rugged lifestyle would suit them."

One evening Peter told his father that he'd found a job opening in Vancouver, Canada. "If I take that teaching position I'll have three summer months of free time. Would you like to have me build you a home this summer up there in the woods?"

Claude liked the idea and plans quickly materialized.

"Mom, I'd love to build a log home for you," Peter lamented, "but it is to be a frame structure, 24' by 36'. Any other ideas or specifications?"

"Yes, build the house without walls in the interior except for the two bedrooms and a bathroom. And I would like a loft with an open stairway."

Surprised, Peter showed me his sketch. He had laid out the space exactly as I had specified. He had designed the house with a cathedral ceiling. I was pleased.

The week before Memorial Day, 1975, Peter with his three teenage brothers, left for the Upper Peninsula, driving an old Chevy pick up truck pulling our little camper loaded with food. He bought a long extension ladder and a wheelbarrow with a box of tools and the adventure began!

Scavenging was in Peter's blood. He didn't waste a penny, but went out to find the most reasonably priced lumber or materials which were free for the hauling. Alvin and John carefully cleaned the mortar off the old bricks from a torn-down gas station and stacked them in neat piles. A friend named John from Grandville, was a good mason and he came to construct the fireplace. An assembly line made the work efficient. Calvin mixed the mortar; Peter carried the supplies to the hard-working John.

As I watched them working so hard, perspiring in the heat, I was overwhelmed to think they were doing all this for us! I stood there, tears welling in my eyes, not knowing what to say, and then I heard Peter holler, "Mom, Don't just stand there! Make us something to eat; we're starved!" He told me where to find a cold spring, two miles down the road so I could make gallons of cold lemonade. Our house wasn't built with just bricks and mortar, it cost food!

In between preparing not three, but five meals a day, I tried to plant a vegetable and flower garden, homesteading our land. One day as I was planting our rows of beans in the red dirt, I remembered my father. Twenty years had passed, and like him, I need to see beans grow. Again I head him say, "Amy, do you know beans will grow anywhere on this planet earth? God made beans to adapt to any climate. It is a comfort to know this!"

My friend, the old Hemlock, stood very close to the corner

of our new home. The workers considered her a nuisance although she was not actually standing in the way. They pushed her branches aside with their trucks and backhoe and I had to plead with them to spare her life. I wondered how she felt about all the activity going on around her and sensed that maybe she was a bit annoyed. Maybe too she was a bit amused as she observed the moods of these young people who laughed, scolded, sang, sighed, argued, teased and agreed. Through it all I was sure she admired them for the love they were pouring into their work.

"Mom, how about a nice deck here on the east side of the house?" Peter asked.

"A deck?"

"Yes, it can be done best now when I put up these beams for a door. Wouldn't it be nice? Dad and you can sit here and look out."

Astonished as I stood there on rubbish, six feet away from trees and brush so thick a bear could be hiding ten feet away and I wouldn't notice, the thought that Claude and I would ever have time to sit together on a deck seemed ridiculous!

Wearily I said, "And look at the woods?" A deck seemed absurd and I began to cry.

"Mom?" Peter asked.

"Oh, forget it," I told him. "This is so big an adventure. You boys work so hard just for Dad and me. We can't ever reward you. Besides, I'm not really sure this is what I want, living here in these strange woods. This will take all the money we have plus more we must borrow."

"Mom, you're missing Dad. You always loved to live in the U.P. It's just your attitude. Be happy! We don't mind all the hard work for you and Dad. You did so much for us."

I dried my tears and looked up to our six foot four son who now lectured and gave me comfort. We had immigrated once, and then I did not know the language of our country. At least I could communicate with U.P. citizens; and yes, Peter was right. I loved to live here where I was close to nature.

The two track road leading off Lake Road about five miles east of LIttle Girls Point was too isolated for a power line, and the cost prohibitive at this point. The constant booming of a generator told me the location of our home going up in nowhere when I ventured out to explore the dense forty acres.

First the foundation was dug out. The basement walls were only five feet high because of the high water level. Then a

Building the House Around the Chimney

friend built a fireplace. The bare chimney pointing to the sky was an awkward sight. Peter told me, "It's like an arm stretching out to help build our home around that towering structure."

The mason friend who built it had only one week to do so, but he did it! The cathedral ceiling and the walls were plastered. The cedar battens were stained a mahogany brown. That was my job. Standing on the makeshift scaffold, I tried to keep my balance...physically as well as mentally. Peter kept calling, "Mom, don't smear the white plaster. You're shaking too much!"

"I'm no steeple jack," I told him.

At last we took pictures of the workmen and the house and then left for home.

In 1976, we spent another happy spring vacation at Eel Lake and visited our new house in the woods. Before we left for home, Calvin looked up at the skeleton of rafters inside. "I'm still tired," he said, remembering the long days of hard work.

A short visit with Mary Young ended the full week of fun. She chattered, babbled, and busily told us, "Gladys is gone! I don't know what happened, but she died suddenly in January. I'm the only survivor of the family now and I will come to see you at Eel Lake and in your new home too."

In the summer of 1978 we moved to our home in the woods. Our house downstate in Grandville sold for five thousand more than we had expected, and with Claude's retirement, our children became eligible for grants, scholarships and loans. We have kept our promise to God to share our house in the woods, and at many times have had some unusual guests!

I was surprised there were so many visitors who found our secluded home. Resting awhile, they usually traveled on but some became friends who returned every year.

The Old Hemlock Shelters Our Home

*Cooking
on the
Woodstove*

*Future
Bach*

Milking Barabra

Loving "Kids"

Pond Creatures

Forest Creatures

Frogs

And
Six Silly Sisters

223

Sara

Lake Superior sighed, her waves falling heavily on shore and her breath ice cold. November rushed to an end, followed by December when she would be singing, accompanied by the music of tiny tinkling little bits of clear blue ice, until it is frozen and still, death still.

I had come to the lake to pick flowers, leftovers from last summer and to gather strands of coarse grasses that had lost their seeds. I meant it to be a bouquet for Sara, my young friend.

She had called me Memmy like our children. That changed when she was a young teen. In a husky voice, she'd say, "Amy," and the warmth in her voice was inherited from her father, Clarence Phillips.

He and Edith, his wife, were our neighbors. They asked me to babysit Sara when she was two years old. When they moved from Cheyenne Drive to the Detroit area, they were our friends, and we always seemed to be on the receiving end.

Yesterday, Sara died, like her father, from a horrible disease called A.L.S., amyotrophic lateral sclerosis, commonly known as Lou Gehrig's disease.

I picked another dead weed that once was a living plant and it seemed right. It had lost its seed. Next summer one of the exact species will sprout and there will be many, many more.

I thought of Clarence running with a watering can, trying to nurse the shoots of wild sweet peas he had transplanted from the riotously blooming ones on the roadside to his twenty virgin acres at Shelby Beach. I had wondered if that dry dune sand had enough nutrients to sustain them and if the roots would take hold. He diligently watered them and placed markers to protect them so that when we came camping in the dunes on the Fourth of July holiday, our rowdy bunch would not trample his sweet peas.

"Look out for Clarence's sweet peas," I warned when we

came to the gate and it became a habitual reminder with all of us chuckling in anticipation of meeting our friends.

They welcomed us with open arms, and Sara was an extension to our family again. She and Judy were closest in age. They soon explored the surrounding area and were gone for hours.

Clarence, well informed about the history and characters that found solace in the dunes around the shore of lake Michigan, often headed an excursion of our older children past the old lighthouse, hoping to find the location where a hermit had printed his own newspaper. The manually operated press was still supposed to be in his shack. The search went on for several years, but sand and time kept the place mysteriously hidden, in contrast to the man's eccentric ideas which the people in the town of Mears still remembered.

I selected another blade of dried grass because its shape looked like that of the long beach grass, planted to keep the dunes from erosion. The roots are deep and they tenaciously grab the soil to find moisture.

I have a picture of our family sitting on the top of a dune watching the sun go down. We had our evening devotions and were singing a hymn. Our campfire was still sputtering on the beach, and the tall grass bowed reverently in a quiet breeze. Clarence and Edith walked along the shore at the water's edge where the sand was firm.

"You didn't go to church tonight?" Clarence asked.

"No, we stayed here and had our own service."

"You should have gone to church," he said.

Clarence did not attend church and I must have looked surprised at his answer.

"Yes!" he said. "You always go to church, Amy."

I understood he was disappointed as if he had lost an opportunity. Our friends cared, hoping that we, without losing our identity, would be happy transplants, taking root.

With every addition to our family, a baby that was born or an adopted child, each one unquestionably received a hearty welcome by the Phillips. When our girls introduced their boyfriends, Clarence scrutinized them seriously, and they were pleased with his approval. It may have been a test for the young man when the girls brought him on a Sunday afternoon to the ridge at "The Property." A wide view of the lake with its sandy beach surprised him, a big plus.

Each summer another tent expanded our camp. The older children paired off for a hike, and Claude and I, wading along the shore, took the younger children to a shallow creek where darting minnows hurriedly swam ahead of splashing little feet until we came to a big dam. The water rushing over it made a waterfall that easily might take one off balance. Claude and the children, holding on to their bathing suits immersed themselves until chilled and then climbed a high dune to have the warm sun dry them.

I tried my luck catching small perch for an evening snack. There were never enough, but a bowl of cereal topped with juicy blackberries was a good compensation for the late comers. Sara and Clarence ate the bulk of the fish. By instinct, they knew to be present for my treat.

Labor Day weekend for me is always sad except for the year when Don gave Anne her engagement ring near the stairs to the ridge. We had a huge campfire built like a teepee. It was also Anne's birthday on the fifth of September and Claude's the third. Clarence and Sara celebrated theirs on the second. I remember Sara saying, "I am my father's birthday present." She said it very seriously and I was not sure what she meant.

For years Sara vacationed with us. It seemed natural that she would come to help Peter build our home in the U.P. of Michigan. It made a great difference. When she arrived, the boys laughed and joked. She carried loads of the rubble they had left behind to a low spot in the woods.

She Came to Help

On her last week here, Peter gave us a few days off, and Sara and I planned to camp in the Sylvania wilderness. Arriving at the Ranger Station, she phoned a friend, giggling and laughing like a girl who is in love. It took some time before she told me. "I'd like to be married someday. My parents are very happy?" She said it as if she questioned me. I did not answer her. Why was she so serious?

It rained steadily for two days and we decided to break camp and spend the night at Eel Lake cabin. By a glowing hot fire, the old cabin logs reflected the flames to a rich copper color. We enjoyed a simple meal of summer squash. Sara had cooked it to perfection, crisp with a sprinkling of cheese and butter; it tasted delicious.

I had not known she had a special friend. Wanting to ask her about her friendship, I hesitated and said, "Sara, what place do you like best? Our home in the forest near Lake Superior or this little cabin at Eel Lake?"

She thought for awhile and then said, "Amy, I feel this place is very good and your home is good too because you may not be selfish."

Her answer was important to me. Her father, Clarence, loaned Peter the money to build our home and he had told Peter, "You must build a good home for your parents. Your mother wouldn't mind living in a small shack if only she can be in the wild forests of the Upper Peninsula!" Her answer made so much sense. I didn't ask more. At one time a sign Claude had carved with our family motto pleased Clarence. His loan was a trusting down payment for what it said; Work, Share, Fun, and in the center, God.

Without specifically selecting each dried weed and dead flower, my bouquet became a wild array of sadness and beauty.

Clarence and Edith were our first visitors to our home on the dirt road near Lake Superior. They were interested in our new adventure, and it surprised me that Clarence so unquestionably accepted our new environment, the forest with hidden waterfalls, the huge rock formations, and our old cabin at Eel Lake. On their last evening, we enjoyed the muted hazy blue and orange sunset at the

Black River harbor. It would be our last visit here together.

Clarence, like so many of the Phillips family, became ill with the disease A.L.S. He wrote:

Dear Amy and Claude,

Edith and I had so much of love, friendship, admiration and yes, a little envy from our relationship with the Vans, especially you, Amy and Claude also but he more recently. I can now reveal Claude, that you have for a long time had another rival for Amy...me.

With death so near, one turns always backward to life and memories of which I have so many that include two warm wonderful persons...the Vans. Your next to the last letter, written in the fullness of your love for and wonder at the glories of nature at Little Girl's Point in the cold, cold winter, was a joyous singing of hymns of praise to your life.

I loved it as I love both of you, it seems so natural to say it now. All you can do for me now is to remain as you are and have been-the complete enjoyers of life and sharers of your enjoyment.

And Claude, you received $500.00 for carving a sign? It probably was worth a $1000! I liked the design even as poorly rendered Amy did. Bees in her bonnet, yes, but art...?

Better than your letters, we like a personal visit with you. Is there anyway you could make a stop over in Detroit on your return from the Netherlands? It is not a commenced performance, but it would be enjoyed by us if you can do it.

I am in fair general health, the weakness and paralysis is spreading up to the left arm. My lungs are stabilized but I have oxygen supply in the house.

I feel sorry for Edith but she sports roads mostly clear of snow.

Clarence

Edith's P.S.

Amy, could you possibly change your route on the way back? I can get you from the airport.

Love, Edith

Clarence died the day after his letter was mailed to us. Yes, I changed my schedule, having been to my father's ninetieth birthday celebration and arrived at Detroit where Edith was waiting for me.

She told me Clarence, on the last evening of his life, had given valuable instructions to a young man, a student at the Lawrence Institute where he was director of the library.

"I am so sorry. He was looking forward to hearing about your trip when he wrote his letter to Claude and you. I thought it quite humorous," she said, "especially picturing you with bees in your bonnet. . . ."

A cold mist blew to shore and drove me from the beach. I carefully arranged my bouquet to mail to Judy, who had promised she would weave a pouch for it and send it on to Edith as a memory for Sara. I thought, "She knew so much of what I did not."

The last time we visited Sara was after our daughter Amy's wedding. We chatted like friends. She limped a little, and in her backpack was a leg brace.

"I may need this soon," she said.

I tried to ignore it but she did not let me.

"At first I thought twenty-six years is too short a lifetime, but now I feel it was worth it," she said.

"Sara, No!"

"I was my father's birthday present; he is gone and now I've no right to live."

"Sara, you must live. You are a continuation of your father's life."

"Amy, I wish that were true, but I feel guilty. Why should his present live when he is not?"

"Sara, I know a man who lost his wife recently from A.L.S. He is going on with life. I wish you would talk to him," I said.

She agreed, and I brought her to our friend, Gerhardt Olson. I left, praying he would give her hope. Gerhardt told her about Jesus and His great love for her. He prayed for Sara and gave her a Bible to read.

When I took her to the airport, my faith was too small, knowing, but not believing that Sara and I would be parting for good.

Sara smiled. "Amy, it is already difficult for me to walk and now I've to carry this heavy Bible too," she said.

"Yes," was all I could say. As so often before, I was not sure what she meant to tell me.

"I've promised Gerhardt Olson to read it and I will," she said, giving me all the comfort I needed.

Edith told me a group of young people from a church in Chicago had cared for Sara. Early in the fall, they brought her to "The Property" at Shelby Beach for a last farewell.

Sara, like her father, passed quietly from this life. She was a present to all of us left behind and no doubt a gift to those in heaven.

On our fortieth wedding anniversary, it was our wish to celebrate with all our children at "The Property" on the beach at Shelby. Edith graciously gave us her cottage for the weekend and then asked if she and her sister Jeanette could share in our happiness. There were no doubt smiles in heaven when all the "Vans" once more sang around a huge camp fire.

A Christmas Tree

We returned from a trip downstate where we celebrated Thanksgiving Day with seven of our children. Their love left a warm glow, captured by the snow covered Christmas decorations illuminating the houses along Lake Road on our way home.

"Claude, soon it will be time for you to cut our tree," I said.

"You want a tree again?" he asked.

"Of course, why not? This year I want one approximately a foot taller than last year. It should reach all the way to the ceiling."

"Why do you want a Christmas tree? None of the children will come home."

Sensing he was stalling me, I said, "I want a tree for myself!"

Year after year we argue about the size of our tree. I want a perfect tree with full dark green branches, a beautiful, soft, fragrant balsam.

At one time when the children were small, Claude, hoping for a bargain, went to the Christmas tree lot on Christmas Eve after most of the trees were sold. He returned with the excited group in tow who happily announced, "Mom, we got this tree for only two dollars. It has a bad side, but Dad told us we can turn that part to the wall."

Grinning at the memories, I said, "Claude, we don't have to bargain or skimp on a tree anymore. There are hundreds growing on your twenty acres across the road."

"Amy, I don't understand you.   All year long you protect our trees. I have to ask you first before I even cut one, near our home. Then at Christmas time you want a tall straight growing tree that I have to take inside to die. Then you decorate that beautiful balsam with glittering junk."

"The man has a cold, factual brain. Why can't he be more

sentimental?" When he left for his shop, I finished wrapping the Christmas presents for the kids.

It was true that last year Claude had to go out four times before he brought me one that satisfied me. The first one was scrawny and slender; it would need lots of ornaments and candy canes to fill up the spaces between branches. The second one had a crooked top, and the third one was too fat and short, but I made good use of them all. One was for the birds, hung with popcorn, bits of suet and cranberries. Mildred Kantala had liked the crooked tree. Her husband wasn't well enough to go out and cut one. I placed the other on the porch. With enough lights and snow covering the branches, it was very pretty. The fourth one was beautiful, a little short, but I placed the stand on a platform and with a lighted star on top, it reached to the ceiling.

Oh no, I was not going to give up! This had been our first disagreement. Men, of course, will never understand women, so I decided to start my Christmas baking. It is a woman's secret allurement to a man's heart.

The section of Christmas goodies in my recipe box is full of sentimental memories of friends. I remembered my father who gave me the recipe for Dutch Butter Banket. My crust never turned out deliciously flaky like his. On "Sinterklaas" Day, Dec. 6, the bishop from Spain arrived on his white horse with Black Peter, his helper bringing presents and a Banket Letter. Our initial, the first letter of my name "Y," regularly broke in transport and was missing one arm. I made my Banket in a straight stick or sometimes a circle and I will gladly share my father's recipe with you.

Crust: Cut one pound butter in four cups flour and
one cup cold water. Roll out on flour dusted
surface. Fold dough in a square four times.
Place in refrigerator to cool. Roll out and fold four
times again. Cool. Do it a third time. Cool.

Filling: Approx. 1 pound almond paste or two cans
Solo almond filling. Blend with one egg and one
cup sugar.

Divide in bowl like a pie in eight slices.
Take crust dough. Divide in eight squares.
Roll out one square at a time to a strip of 8 inches
by 4 inches on heavily flour dusted board. Roll by
hand on board one of the eight prepared almond
paste unto the strip of crust. Fold crust loosely
around the paste. Brush the end with milk and it will
hold. Pinch the ends (heel) of theroll. Brush with
egg yolk thinned with a little milk. Sprinkle with
sugar or garnish with colored pieces of cherries.
Bake at 325 degrees to 350 degrees until golden
brown. Four rolls will fit lengthwise on a regular
cookie sheet in the center of top of the oven.

"Smakelyk Eeten!" Eat with delight!

A good cup of coffee with a two inch slice of Banket roll is a temptation no man will resist.

"Claude, don't you love me enough to cut me a tall tree?" I asked. "Don't wade through deep snow to your twenty. The one in front of your shop is about the right size. You can cut it to approximately fourteen feet and I will use the bottom branches in the flower boxes."

In turn he asked me, "Don't you love me enough for me to want a cute small tree?"

Well, after fifty years of marriage, he is still as stubborn as the day I met him, I thought. It does not make sense to argue at a time when the world sings about peace.

Reflecting on Christmases past comes easily when baking cookies. Thoughts mingle with the aroma of cinnamon, allspice and ginger, and shaping the stars, bells, angels and trees.

I pictured our children long ago when I frosted the cookies myself and they decorated them with silver pills and colored sugar.

"Don't overdo it," I warned. "Those are for the visitors. But you may make two for yourself to eat now." They loaded those with silver, red and green decorations, and it would probably mean another expensive visit to the dentist.

Claude had told the children not to make that long trip to

visit us in the U.P. this winter, and he was right. We had a wonderful time on Thanksgiving. And in March, on the way to Florida, we would see everyone again. But it would be awfully quiet this Christmas. At least there was no need to pray for a safe journey those six hundred miles up and then traveling downstate again through possible snow and sleet. And our children established their own family holiday traditions with students coming home from college and taking their friends home.

But I wanted a nice tall Christmas tree like all the other years and wouldn't give in yet!

The candy canes might not mysteriously disappear with the brightly colored chocolate balls, like other years. In my mind, I saw children singing around the tree and reciting their parts in the Sunday School program. Why can't Christmas be celebrated in July? I thought. At that time of the year, everyone likes to visit and we can accommodate many. They love to camp at Little Girl's Point.

"There's nothing as good as waking up in the morning near Lake Superior, drinking a good cup of coffee, and looking out at the Porcupine Mountains," one of our girls once told me.

Aimless and lazy, a few snowflakes dwindled past the window. More followed, tumbling now faster and faster, chasing each other from a gray sky. What would Christmas be without snow here in the U.P.? And what would Christmas be without angels singing good-will toward men... in a mad world or of shepherds worshiping and wise men taking gifts to a Christ Child who was born to pay for our sins. God's love was shining down from heaven on Him and as well on me today, a bright star guiding me through life!

God knows we have also had Christmas times when the light was dim with heartaches, which now we know, He graciously turned into blessings and loving miracles saying, "I will do great and marvelous things of which you do not know." I remembered when Anne was nearly killed coming home from a music lesson in Muskegon a few days before Christmas. That Monday morning long ago, while watering my plants, a foreboding anxiety brought a dripping tear down my cheek onto a flower. Wiping it, I heard the phone ring.

Someone said, "Mrs. Van Ooyen, your daughter has had an accident. I'm calling from the emergency room at St. Mary's Hospital in Grand Rapids."

Instinctively preparing, I called Claude at work and asked him to meet me at the hospital and then asked my neighbor to watch the little children. I then called our minister.

Claude met me at the hospital at the same time. Our pastor was speeding down the Beltline and he had told me, "Amy, if it is the Lord's will to take Anne, you must let her go."

"No, never, we are a unit. Our children all have special gifts and talents. When one is gone, our family is not complete. You preached yesterday about faith, that we are tried but never defeated," I said.

Claude and I watched Anne, convulsive and fighting for her life when they took her to the Intensive Care unit. We waited and waited in the same room where a woman, silent and resigned, also waited.

She spoke in a quiet voice, tired and spent saying, "My son lies so still and in a coma, the doctors have not given us much hope."

Doctors and nurses hurried down the corridor. The swinging doors of the I.C. Unit opened and shut, decorated with an oversized waving and smiling fat Santa.

Every time the door opened, we expected to hear from our doctor. I could not wait anymore and didn't know what to pray. Someone gave me a pamphlet with a short poem I have forgotten, except that it said, "If you can't pray, there are others who will."

Finally, a doctor came asking the quiet lady to follow him. When she returned to the hall, she walked, quietly sobbing, behind a stretcher with her dead son. On the door closing behind them, the broad smiling Santa waved good-bye to them, Ho! Ho! Ho! Ever since, I hate to see a large or even a small picture of Santa.

Anne's vital signs were stabilized but her body was broken in too many places. "She is unconscious, although fortunately not brain damaged," the doctor said.

Three days later, her specialist told us, "All she needs now is to heal her fractures in both legs and arm. We trust Anne will be well someday, but it will take months."

It took almost a year. The outpouring of loving concern of neighbors gave us the much needed courage and strength to cope with our family demands.

Our little town prayed for Anne. Catholic friends burned candles and prayed with Protestants. The Calvin College student body also had a prayer vigil for their classmate. They brought food and washed our clothes. We received anonymous monetary gifts. Then one night I came home from the hospital and a brightly lit Christmas tree loaded with gifts underneath it surprised me.

On that afternoon, the woman who had lost her son came to the hospital. "I've come to thank you, hoping to find you here," she said, hugging me. "Will your daughter be well?" she asked.

We wept together and the heavy knot I carried in my chest dissolved in tears. "And you?" I said.

"My husband and I have another son just like him," she smiled sadly and then said as if she was comforting me, "This younger son will go fishing and hunting with him too."

She left crying a little. We haven't met again, and yet this woman has been an example of love for me and sometimes I have envied her quiet courage.

At lunchtime, I said, "Claude, will you cut me that little Balsam tree that grows near the sauna?"

"Sure," he said. "Do you want it now?"

"You may leave it on the porch. It is crowding the others." He dragged it into the kitchen where it smelled pungent and fresh like a tall one. After cutting the lower branches for the flower boxes, a beautiful symmetric top was left, a perfect miniature Christmas tree that fit into a clay pot woven in a macrame hanger near the stairs.

When Claude returned from his shop, he said, "Are you decorating the tree?"

"Yes, and I'm almost finished." Having chosen my most precious ornaments, the small tree with tiny lights was now a gem of sentiment.

"This is a perfect solution, very practical. I like it," he said.

I had almost expected that he would rush to the woods and get one of the tallest trees, but that was not what I really wanted him to do. He gave me a big hug.

One afternoon the mailman parked his car at the door, passing up our mailbox at the end of the drive and delivered boxes with presents. One of the children wrote, "You will receive a 'family' present too, but we couldn't pass up a few small gifts." These were specially chosen and reflected our interest and their love. The larger family gift was still a secret and would be delivered before Christmas.

I hoped it was something practical, but Claude thought our children had different ideas. "Maybe a computer, they've been telling me about e-mail."

"That's something for you to play with. My pen writes yet," I said.

On Christmas Eve, Claude played the organ for two candlelight services, and when we left home, our present had still not arrived. We kept the door unlocked.

When we returned, a large white envelope lay on the doormat. It said in heavy block letters, "MUST BE DELIVERED BY DEC 24 TH."

Claude hurriedly opened it and a certificate and large Christmas card with a gold text fell out.

My Spirit who is in you,

and my words that

I have put in your mouth

will not depart from your mouth

or from the mouths

of your children.

Isaiah 50:21

I read and smiled. The certificate designed by our daughter Amy also had a message. "This coupon entitles our Dad and Mom, Grandpa and Grandma to the sum of $$$$$. Volunteer labor will be given by children able to come up during the summer of 1996. Probably in the month of July. A very Merry Christmas and Happy New Year. Love, Your kids."

In July, twenty-one children and grandchildren delivered our present, coming from the East, West, and in between. They replaced the roofing on our house and, with the help of our friends, Dave and Carol, cut and stacked forty cords of firewood for the winter.

Gallons of ice cream topped with strawberries from the garden encouraged the crew. They kept working in a scorching heat wave that nearly blistered their knees on the black shingled roof. A dip in the cold clear water of Lake Superior revived them again; and in the evening, we had a picnic with a campfire at Little Girl's Point campground. We experienced a miracle of love. It was "Christmas in July!"

Christmas in July
The Work Crew

238

Ascension Day

I did not plant the beans like you do Dad, three in a hole approximately six inches apart.

Forgive me, Dad. Here in America we plant beans in a row, two inches or so in between so we don't crowd the roots.

Today is Ascension Day and I remembered you waking me at six a.m. We drank a cup of tea. Mine had been sweetened with lots of sugar and you added milk. We drank hot tea, slurping it carefully and we didn't talk, afraid we would break our special moment and shatter our spell.

Ascension Day, the official Christian holiday, a day of heaven as much as of earth. For us, you and I, earth came first at six o'clock in the morning before church at nine a.m.

Not until after you, Dad, took the polished worn spade and checked it for rust spots, would you say, "I take care of my tools, and the fat of a pig's genitals is still the best preservative." For good measure you'd give it a few more strokes with the greasy balls and drape the rope holding that mysterious cure on a rusty nail. "Every time I use my spade, I give it a lick before putting it away," you said.

It never rained on Ascension Day, at least not early in the morning. An old man had tilled the garden by hand. It was a tradition. I guess he needed some extra cash.

Dad, you let me carry the manila bag with seed, and I watched you string a cord for a straight line. Then you swiftly dug a small hole. One scoop of rich black dirt crumbled next to it and you counted three beans in my hand. "Now, drop three beans in every hole, Amy," you'd say.

For years Mother's older sister, Tante Aaltje, who cared for Grandma, had been my Mom. I must have been almost six years old before I returned home and was to begin school. "Your mother didn't feel well," was my father's explanation when I had asked

239

him the reason for our long separation. Much later I understood why you gave me extra attention. You made up for time lost, like me helping you to plant beans on Ascension Day, just us, before church and before the festive celebration in the afternoon of choirs and bands competing in nearby parks.

Ascension Day in the lowlands behind the North Sea dikes was a wonderful day of celebrating "Heaven and Earth"! Ascension Day was a promise, a day for burying beans and waiting for Pentecost ten days later. By nine o'clock, church began with a song and a prayer; and in the afternoon songs, loud trumpets, and music filled the day.

Hadn't Dad told me he found my mother, picking her out as the most beautiful girl singing in one of the choirs and that ten days later, on Pentecost Monday, she promised to become his steady girl?

I counted three beans in each hole. It was difficult. Those beans were slippery.

Ascension Day is sometimes early and sometimes late, like this year. There's no doubt with bowed heads my beans will solemnly rise unfolding their promises. Planted early or late, I've never been disappointed.

And today with memories and a tribute to you, Dad, I planted a straight row of beans, approximately two inches apart. Forgive me.

Then why did I plant three beans in a hole on the end of the row? One for you? One for me? One for those who plant after me?

The Old Hemlock 1997

*H*er branches quivering in anticipation of summer were chanting a new melody and in between her knobby scarred feet, the melting snow left puddles for a little chickadee to take a quick sip. Calling its name, Chic-a-Dee-Dee, extending it with a charming mating song, it flew up on one of her dead branches.

My Hemlock chuckled and laughed when she told me whispering, "Listen, Shuss, Listen!"

Looking up at her battered branches I asked, "Why should I listen to you? What makes you so happy?"

"Shuss, shuss, take time to listen."

"For twenty years, I've been your friend. You are constantly asking me to listen. Where have you been but here, and what do you have to say, old Hemlock? I've been transplanted too many times and I'm tired, fearing one more change," I said.

She invited me to sit on a soft pillow of moss near her roots that were showing scars of decay, a reminder of damage done by reckless men clearing a building site for our home.

With the sun warming my bones after a long cold winter, I leaned comfortably against her rough trunk.

In a soft breeze tossing a chill against my cheeks, she spoke, now quietly, "Listen! Listen, to my music."

I listened with a smile recognizing she was fooling me.

"You are playing tricks again. I don't understand Bach's intricate compositions. Claude comprehends his bewildering music. It is refreshing to his spirit and thrills his soul."

"Oooh, oooh, oh." Mischievously sighing, she waited for my response.

"What is the secret of your happiness? Didn't you groan when your bark split open in below zero temperatures and was not one of your stronger limbs broken under the weight of three hundred inches of snow? Has this past winter not been tough on you? Tell me why I should listen to your music when your wounds haven't healed?" I asked.

"I don't have all the answers. You talk too much and ask too many questions. Shuss. Shuss, listen once more, my friend."

A squalling wind rushed from the shores of Lake Superior, and in the force of a late spring storm, my Hemlock lifted her fresh agile branches that had replaced a broken crown. In a mighty hymn, a swelling chorus, she gave praise for a long happy life.

Beginning to understand her great faith, I asked, "Are Bach's chorales inspiring you too?"

"No, God is! I talk to Him. Listen."

> *I lift my eyes to the hills-*
> *where does my help come*
> *from?*
> *My help comes from the*
> *Lord,*
> *the Maker of heaven and*
> *earth.*
> *He will not let your foot slip-*
> *he who watches over you*
> *will not slumber;*
> *indeed, he who watches over Israel*
> *will neither slumber nor sleep.*
> *The Lord watches over you-*
> *the Lord is your shade at*
> *your right hand;*
> *the sun will not harm you by day,*
> *nor the moon by night.*
> *The Lord will keep you from*
> *from all harm-*
> *he will watch over your life;*
> *The Lord will watch over*
> *your coming and going*
> *both now and forevermore.*

There at her gnarled feet, beneath her broken branches, I received the answer to all my questions.

1998 at Eel Lake

A loon's melancholy wail at the end of a beautiful day is the reminder for me that this book must come to a finish.

Counting our twenty grandchildren, the story of our family is spanning five generations.

During the fifty years of our marriage, Claude and I had a busy life with work, sharing, fun and keeping God in the center of our home. We are blessed.

More could have been told about travel to Europe and the Orient, remote islands in the Pacific Ocean, visits in the royal palaces and mansions with Mrs. Bertha Holt in Thailand and the Philippines, and my wandering in the jungles with faithful missionaries.

I observed poverty in the slums and admired those who were sacrificing their lives, showing compassion by word and deed.

I placed orphaned babies in the arms of loving parents in the United States and Europe and collected ten thousand diapers annually to keep the little bottoms of several hundred babies in Korean orphanages comfortable.

Here at the old cedar log cabin near a little lake in the forest, God gave me a place and time to reflect on the past.

I came to the realization that the honor of receiving a "Mother of the Year" award in our hometown of Grandville is insignificant since every good experience is a gift and all the difficult days were given for our good.

And by God's plan, we are transplants.

My Best Reward
Placing a Baby in the Arms of a Mother in Oslo

In Bangkok

244

With Manguan Tribe
In the Jungle of a
Philipine Island

The Parsonage at Safa
Where We Stayed

John, Calvin, Jane, Judy, Peter, Mom, Dad, Alvin, Ellie, Amy, Kathy, Anne

"Our Motto"

Here is Music
the Trees Talk ...
Promises...
God is Here...

During the last eight years, I have written four books with the help of one special friend, R. Charles Gage Van Riper PhD. Many others have assisted me. The three books I have written about the splendor and wonder of the Upper Peninsula Superior region are:

Live it U.P.!

Now and Then in the U.P.

Creatures and Characters in the U.P.

The books will acquaint you with our neighbors, our simple, happy and often humorous lifestyles and our love for people and nature. These are available at the following address or your local bookstore.

Amy J. Van Ooyen
Woodpecker Books Press
N13508 Partridge Road
Ironwood, Michigan 49938